Cambridge Elements

Elements in the Philosophy of Ludwig Wittgenstein
edited by
David G. Stern
University of Iowa

AF601519

WITTGENSTEIN AND SOCIAL EPISTEMOLOGY

Annalisa Coliva
University of California, Irvine

CAMBRIDGE UNIVERSITY PRESS

Shaftesbury Road, Cambridge CB2 8EA, United Kingdom

One Liberty Plaza, 20th Floor, New York, NY 10006, USA

477 Williamstown Road, Port Melbourne, VIC 3207, Australia

314–321, 3rd Floor, Plot 3, Splendor Forum, Jasola District Centre, New Delhi – 110025, India

103 Penang Road, #05–06/07, Visioncrest Commercial, Singapore 238467

Cambridge University Press is part of Cambridge University Press & Assessment, a department of the University of Cambridge.

We share the University's mission to contribute to society through the pursuit of education, learning and research at the highest international levels of excellence.

www.cambridge.org
Information on this title: www.cambridge.org/9781009551328

DOI: 10.1017/9781009551311

© Annalisa Coliva 2025

This publication is in copyright. Subject to statutory exception and to the provisions of relevant collective licensing agreements, no reproduction of any part may take place without the written permission of Cambridge University Press & Assessment.

When citing this work, please include a reference to the DOI 10.1017/9781009551311

First published 2025

A catalogue record for this publication is available from the British Library

ISBN 978-1-009-55132-8 Hardback
ISBN 978-1-009-55134-2 Paperback
ISSN 2632-7112 (online)
ISSN 2632-7104 (print)

Cambridge University Press & Assessment has no responsibility for the persistence or accuracy of URLs for external or third-party internet websites referred to in this publication and does not guarantee that any content on such websites is, or will remain, accurate or appropriate.

For EU product safety concerns, contact us at Calle de José Abascal, 56, 1°, 28003 Madrid, Spain, or email eugpsr@cambridge.org

Wittgenstein and Social Epistemology

Elements in the Philosophy of Ludwig Wittgenstein

DOI: 10.1017/9781009551311
First published online: August 2025

Annalisa Coliva
University of California, Irvine

Author for correspondence: Annalisa Coliva, a.coliva@uci.edu

Abstract: The last twenty years have witnessed a 'social turn' in analytic philosophy. Social epistemology has been crucial to it. Social epistemology starts by repudiating the kind of individualistic epistemology, which, since Descartes' *Meditations* and through Kant's maxim 'Think for yourself', has dominated philosophy. It is a sign of the deep erasure of Wittgenstein's ideas from many debates in analytic philosophy that neither his views against fundamental tenets of individualistic epistemology, nor his positive contribution to key themes in social epistemology are considered.

This Element on *Wittgenstein and Social Epistemology* is the first comprehensive study of the implications of the later Wittgenstein's ideas for key issues at the core of present-day social epistemology, such as the nature of common sense and its relations to common knowledge; testimony and trust; deep disagreements in connection with genealogical challenges; and the meaning of 'woman' and the role of self-identification in the determination of gender.

This Element also has a video abstract:
www.cambridge.org/EPLW_Coliva_abstract

Keywords: Wittgenstein, social epistemology, feminist philosophy, disagreement, trust

© Annalisa Coliva 2025

ISBNs: 9781009551328 (HB), 9781009551342 (PB), 9781009551311 (OC)
ISSNs: 2632-7112 (online), 2632-7104 (print)

Contents

Typographical Notice

In quotations from Wittgenstein the bold font has been used to indicate emphases added by me to differentiate them from Wittgenstein's original italicized terms. Words in small caps refer to concepts.

1 Wittgenstein and the 'Social Turn' in Contemporary Epistemology

> It is not possible that there should have been only one occasion on which only one person followed a rule. . . . To follow a rule, to make a report, to give an order, to play a game of chess, are *customs* (usages, institutions)
>
> (PI 199)

> That's why 'following a rule' is a practice. And to *think* one is following a rule is not to follow a rule. And that's why it's not possible to follow a rule 'privately'; otherwise, thinking one was following a rule would be the same thing as following it.
>
> (PI 202)

The last twenty years have witnessed a veritable 'social turn' in analytic philosophy. A key role has been played, in this context, by the rise of social epistemology. Virtually all presentations of social epistemology start with the claim that key to social epistemology is the repudiation of the kind of individualistic epistemology, which, since Descartes' *Meditations* and through Kant's maxim 'Think for yourself', has dominated philosophical debates. Individualistic epistemology considers subjects as autonomous inquirers, who acquire knowledge independently of their social and political contexts. It also enjoins them to embark in a process of examination of their own beliefs to determine which, if any, amount to knowledge or are indeed certain. The epistemic credentials of one's beliefs are then traced back either to sense data, manifested in one's private mental arena, or to a priori truths, knowable by reason alone independently of its material situatedness, like the Cartesian cogito, or the Kantian categories. Once again, these foundational items are either available only within the mind of each subject, and known to them in a privileged way, or are nonetheless independent from the interactions with one's peers and from the complexities of the social world in which one lives.

1.1 The Rejection of Individualistic Epistemology in the Later Wittgenstein

It is curious, and a sign of the deep erasure of (the later) Wittgenstein's ideas from many current debates in analytic philosophy, that in the context of the contemporary rejection of this overarching model, his views are not routinely presented as the most radical break with all fundamental tenets of individualistic epistemology.

Many of Wittgenstein's insights prove to be fatal to key tenets of individualistic epistemology. For instance, his conception of meaning as use, in the *Philosophical Investigations*, stresses the ineliminable role of the community not only for language acquisition but also for determining rules, meanings, and, with them, the concepts which we deploy in thought (*contra* the Kantian transcendental model), and opens up to their cultural and historical variability (*contra* Kantian universalist pretensions). His rejection of the very possibility of a private language, whose meanings should putatively be private experiences, stands against the Cartesian model of the mental, as well as the empiricist appeal to sense data as the source of all our concepts. His rejection of the very idea that we may have privileged knowledge of our own mental states – due to their observation within one's own mental arena – and no knowledge of other people's mental states, goes against any form of solipsism; his emphasis on the instinctive and embodied expression of the mental, which is key for acquiring psychological concepts and the ability to attribute them to oneself and others, goes against individualistic models of self-knowledge and of knowledge of other minds. Finally, his rejection (mostly in the *Blue Book*[1]) of the Cartesian idea of the self as a mental substance, and of the Kantian idea that the self is a mere condition of possibility of experience and thought, let alone a bundle of sensations or memories, as Hume and Locke respectively held, in favour of the idea that when 'I' refers at all, it refers to an embodied entity, are all further blows to essential tenets of individualistic epistemology.

Wittgenstein's later writings were also relevant for the development of disciplines in the social sciences. In anthropology, for instance, the *Remarks on Frazer's* The Golden Bough (1993) were crucial for the rejection of James George Frazer's positivistic methodology. Wittgenstein's *Lectures on Religious Belief* (1966), his several remarks in *Culture and Value* (1980) as well as in *On Certainty* (1969), inspired a new approach to the understanding and study of religion. His ideas contributed to the rejection of positivism in sociology, also thanks to Peter Winch's *The Idea of Social Science and Its Relation to Philosophy* (1958); and, owing to Barry Barnes and David Bloor's (1996) *Scientific Knowledge: A Sociological Analysis*, they contributed to the development of the so-called 'strong programme' in the sociology of science. Finally, Wittgenstein's idea of language-games and rule-governed practices were key for the development of game theory.

[1] There is already a brief rejection of this idea in TLP 5.631.

1.2 The Rejection of Individualistic Epistemology in *On Certainty*

Yet, it is in *On Certainty* that the relevance of Wittgenstein's ideas to contemporary social epistemology becomes even more obvious.[2] For the key contention is that all inquiry revolves around 'hinges' (OC 341–343) – that is, propositions that have an empirical form and yet are removed from doubt and investigation. By staying put, they allow 'the door to turn'. That is, they allow us to form justification for, and possibly gain knowledge of ordinary empirical propositions. As he writes in those key passages:

> That is to say, the *questions* that we raise and our *doubts* depend on the fact that some propositions are exempt from doubt, are as it were like hinges on which those turn.
>
> That is to say, it belongs to the logic of our scientific investigations that certain things are *in deed* not doubted.
>
> But it isn't that the situation is like this: We just *can't* investigate everything, and for that reason we are forced to rest content with assumption. If I want the door to turn, the hinges must stay put.

For instance, it's only by taking for granted that the Earth has existed for a very long time that we can take fossils to bear on the determination of the age of the Earth. If we didn't take that for granted, then the presence of those fossils would have no bearing on the inquiry into the age of the Earth, as it would be compatible with the Earth's having popped into existence only recently, replete with everything we find on it.

Unlike Descartes, who in his *First Meditation* seeks to question all his prior beliefs to identify what withstands doubt and can serve as a secure foundation for the rational reconstruction of knowledge, Wittgenstein maintains that doubt arises only after belief[3] (OC160) and does not serve as a means of attaining either knowledge or certainty. That is, rational doubt is possible, for Wittgenstein, only by taking hinges for granted. Thanks to them, we can then acquire reasons against specific j/k-apt beliefs – that is, beliefs that are either justified or known.[4] Hyperbolic, global doubts are necessarily unmotivated by reasons, since they call into question the hinges that make it possible to acquire reasons for and against ordinary empirical propositions. Being unmotivated by reasons, they breach the criteria for meaningful doubt and are, in fact, a mere

---

[2] *Contra* Hertzberg (1988: 307–308) who, however, also points out the essential role of trust – and hence of our social interconnectedness – in OC, and stresses the deeply social dimension of Wittgenstein's reflections on meaning in PI, which are in the background of OC.

[3] 'Belief' here is belief in hinges, which unlike 'j/k-apt belief', isn't supported by reasons and apt to become knowledge when true and justified.

[4] 'Belief' is an umbrella term, which spans across beliefs that can be supported by reasons and become justified or known, up to beliefs that aren't so apt, and are mostly an expression of faith or trust. We will come back to this issue in Section 3.

illusion of doubt. As Wittgenstein puts it in OC (450): 'A doubt that doubted everything would not be a doubt'.

Furthermore, the metaphysical possibilities raised by Cartesian sceptical scenarios are ultimately nonsensical for Wittgenstein (OC 383, 676), although certainly deserving of careful investigation (OC 37). Outside their ordinary employment, in contexts of sensory and cognitive disconnect, sentences like 'It's raining' or even 'I am dreaming' cannot refer to events in the world, even if it is raining outside or one is indeed dreaming. Rather, they may only refer to the dream of the rain or to the dream of dreaming. Thus, the Cartesian sceptical hypothesis, encapsulated in the phrase 'I am dreaming', doesn't express any truly conceivable possibility: if I am dreaming of it, it cannot describe the situation I am in, but, at most, only my dreaming of it, in which case it shouldn't worry us any more than dreaming of the rain should worry us about getting wet.[5] If, in contrast, 'I am dreaming' is thought of or asserted while being awake, it is false, and easily disproved by the application of ordinary criteria of verification.

Hinges, furthermore, have the form of empirical propositions, or, more precisely, are propositions about ordinary material objects (OC 401–402) or parts of physical bodies, like hands and feet, or tables and chairs; animals and plants, like cats and trees; chemical compounds, like water, as well as planets and celestial bodies like the Earth, the Moon, and the Sun. In some cases, they are propositions grounded in habit and memory, like 'My name is . . . ', and they mostly depend on being enculturated within a certain form of life.

The relevance of this observation is that at the foundation of all our thinking, for Wittgenstein, there are neither propositions about sense data, contrary to the empiricists (OC 90, 426), nor solely a priori truths, let them be the Cartesian cogito, or logical or mathematical propositions (OC 303–306, 651), or a priori categories. Indeed, a key aim of *On Certainty* is to go past the received view and claim that just as we don't call into doubt a priori truths, and keep them firm against all possible counterevidence, so we don't call hinges into doubt and, at least in context, don't admit of contrary evidence. As Wittgenstein writes in OC (340): 'We know, **with the same certainty with which we believe *any* mathematical proposition**, how the letters A and B are pronounced, what the colour of human blood is called, that other human beings have blood and call it "blood"'.[6]

In both cases this is due, for Wittgenstein, to the role these diverse propositions play in our communal epistemic practices. As Wittgenstein writes in OC (655, 657):

[5] Even more radically, for Wittgenstein, in the context of a dream, those words would only retain an appearance of meaning. This may escape notice because we tend to project it back from the contexts of their ordinary employment. (Cf. OC 10, 348).

[6] We will return to Wittgenstein's use of 'I know' and 'to know' in connection with hinges in Section 2.

> The mathematical proposition has, as it were officially, been given the stamp of incontestability. I.e.: "Dispute about other things; *this is* immovable – it is a hinge on which your dispute can turn."
>
> The propositions of mathematics might be said to be **fossilized**. The proposition "I am called . . . " is not. But it too is regarded as *incontrovertible* by those who, like myself, have overwhelming evidence for it. And this is not out of thoughtlessness. For, the evidence's being overwhelming consists precisely in the fact that we do not *need* to give way before any contrary evidence. **And so we have here a buttress similar to the one that makes the propositions of mathematics incontrovertible**.

Interestingly, moreover, the certainty enjoyed by our psychological avowals, for Wittgenstein, is not itself a function of a privileged and infallible access that subjects putatively have to their own mental states. Rather, it is the result of our communal, linguistic practice, in which subjects are accorded authority over their own mental states, at least *ceteris paribus* (i.e., provided there is no reason to suspect deceit or conceptual impairment). In *Philosophical Investigations* Wittgenstein writes (PI 247–248):

> "Only you can know if you had that intention." One might tell someone this when one was explaining the meaning of the word "intention" to him. For then it means: that is how we use it. (**And here "know" means that the expression of uncertainty is senseless.**)
>
> The proposition "Sensations are private" is comparable to: "One plays patience by oneself".

It is a grammatical remark, for Wittgenstein, and therefore an outcome of our linguistic practice, that people are accorded authority over their own mental states, which, in turn, are conceptualized in such a way that they are not taken to be intersubjectively manifest. Consequently, 'Only you can know . . . ' with respect to them is a grammatical remark that reminds us that, in virtue of that very practice, a third party's doubt or uncertainty about the fact that one is in pain, or has a certain intention, when one avows those mental states, is excluded from the language-game, at least *ceteris paribus* (i.e., if there is no reason to think they may be deceitful or conceptually impaired).

Once more, this should make us realize that the various items that traditional epistemological projects have posited as sitting at the foundations of all human knowledge and as inherently certain, are in no way special. All certainties – also the ones that have long been thought to be the outcome of individualistic investigations and to pertain to private realms, like the mental, or to be accessible only by means of a priori reflections, like mathematical ones – are in fact a function of the role they play within human linguistic and epistemic practices.

Thus, as we saw, hinges are typically acquired through enculturation within a shared form of life and are by no means the outcomes of solitary inquiry, contrary to the tenets of individualistic epistemology. Hinges, however, are many and diverse, for Wittgenstein. As he writes: 'And the bank of that river consists partly of hard rock, subject to no alteration or only to an imperceptible one, partly of sand, which now in one place now in another gets washed away, or deposited' (OC 99).

Hence, some hinges stay put over time and cultures. For instance, we take it for granted that the Earth has existed for a very long time, and that it was inhabited by our ancestors well before us. Of course, the precise age of the Earth has been a topic of heated debate, but not the hinge proposition that the Earth has been existing for a long time.

Some other hinges, however, may and do change over time (OC 96–98, 336). Thus, what we consider to be justified/able (and therefore known/able) is not given once and for all but inextricably depends on our historical, and social situatedness. One of Wittgenstein's examples is 'Nobody has ever been on the Moon',[7] and he considers examples of propositions which used to play a hinge-like role – for example 'The Earth is flat' – for which contrary evidence was either ignored or explained away, that no longer play a hinge-like role for us. Writes Wittgenstein (OC 96–97):[8]

> It might be imagined that some propositions, of the form of empirical propositions, were hardened and functioned as channels for such empirical propositions as were not hardened but fluid; and that this relation altered with time, in that fluid propositions hardened, and hard ones became fluid.
>
> The mythology may change back into a state of flux, the river-bed of thoughts may shift. But I distinguish between the movement of the waters on the river-bed and the shift of the bed itself; though there is not a sharp division of the one from the other.

Still, according to Wittgenstein, and contrary to W.v.O. Quine's (1951) later rejection of the analytic/synthetic distinction in 'Two dogmas of empiricism', at every moment or relative to any given context, we may distinguish between propositions that play a hinge-like role and those which don't, even though at a different time, or in a different context, the former may become empirical ones, and the latter may be hardened into rules. As he writes (OC 98):

> But if someone were to say "So logic too is an empirical science" he would be wrong. Yet this is right: the same proposition may get treated at one time as something to test by experience, at another as a rule of testing.

---

[7] OC was composed between 1949 and 1951, thus about twenty years before the moon landing.

[8] In Coliva (2025), I distinguish between de jure and de facto hinges. Some of the differences between these two kinds of hinge are discussed in Section 2.

Yet, to reiterate, hinges are typically acquired by being part of a linguistic and epistemic community. We don't have them thanks to the pursuit of a personal quest for certainty, let alone one that accords pride of place to the deliverances of introspection or of purely a priori reasoning. On the contrary, as Wittgenstein puts it, they are the 'inherited background' against which we distinguish between true and false (OC 94). Thus, neither inquiry nor knowledge would be possible for isolated subjects. Clearly, then, the rejection of the main tenets of individualistic epistemology, with its psychologistic or purely a priori underpinnings, is an overarching theme of Wittgenstein's later philosophy and particularly of *On Certainty*. To repeat, for him, at the foundations of our thinking and inquiring there are, rather, propositions about material objects, which are susceptible to change over time, and which are part of an inherited world-picture (*Weltbild*, OC 93–95, 162, 167, 233, 262).

1.3 Wittgenstein and the Critical Dimension of Social Epistemology

So far, we have considered, in very general terms, the contribution of Wittgenstein's later writings to anti-individualistic epistemology. There is, however, another aspect to the 'social turn' in contemporary analytic philosophy: a growing focus, particularly led by feminist epistemologists, on social structures and differences, especially those related to power and privilege.

In this connection too, the later Wittgenstein has – perhaps surprisingly – something to teach us. I say 'perhaps surprisingly' because his 'quietism' – that is, the view that in philosophy we cannot advance theses and that 'all *explanation* must disappear, and description alone must take its place' (PI 109) – is often considered to make his views unserviceable in the context of politically charged issues, characteristic of feminist epistemology, or within the contemporary wave of 'ameliorative' projects in philosophy of mind and language.

However, thanks especially to Naomi Scheman's pioneering work (Scheman 2011, but see also Scheman and O'Connor 2002, Code 1991, Tanesini 2004, O'Connor 2008, Ashton 2019, and Laugier, Provost, and Trächtler 2022), Wittgenstein's ideas have been rallied to the feminist cause. More recently, thanks to Anna Boncompagni's work (2019, 2024 a, b), as well as to Danièle Moyal-Sharrock and Constantine Sandis (2004) and Coliva (2025a, d, 2025), *On Certainty* and some ideas in the later Wittgenstein have been brought to bear on various forms of epistemic injustice (Fricker 2007), and on discussions about gender and trans identities (Stoljar 1995, 2011, Hay 2020, Coliva 2025a).

More generally, the later Wittgenstein continuously asks us to imagine *alternative* practices, epistemic or otherwise. Consider the famous case of the odd wood sellers in *The Remarks on the Foundations of Mathematics* (Wittgenstein 1956 I, 59) with their alternative epistemic practice of measuring the quantity of wood and of paying for it[9]; or the case of the builders in the *Philosophical Investigations*, with their partially different language-games; or the different forms of life he asks us to imagine – let them be biologically different ones (PI II 223e), or only culturally different ones (OC 92, 132).

These exercises in imagination have the role of exposing the contingent nature of our epistemic practices, language-games, and forms of life. They aim at debunking the idea that there are essences and metaphysical necessities at every corner where we are normally tempted to see them. Rather, once tested through imagination, alleged essences, or metaphysical necessities, often turn out to be projections of our way of operating with language and thought. To the extent that such an essentialist conception of reality is shared by lay members of the community, becoming able to see it for what it is – that is, merely a projection of our categories and practices onto reality – can be a liberating skill for philosophers to share with the rest of their community. That is, Wittgenstein's own methodology can be a powerful ally in the context of philosophical and critical world-building. Yet, Wittgenstein is also unsympathetic to the idea that if something is merely imaginable it should be taken into account to understand our extant concepts and practices.

What some Wittgenstein-inspired feminists have noticed (particularly Scheman 2011) is that looking at materially different forms of life, or even at the heterogeneity of a single form of life – especially on the margins, where 'mixed, nonbinary, interstitial, complex, contested, unclear identities' emerge and 'invite rethinking our existing categories' (Boncompagni and Coliva 2024: 1) – can have a similarly liberating effect, while overcoming Wittgenstein's own scepticism regarding the possibility of imagining radically different forms of life. Furthermore, endorsing the cause of the marginalized could help bring about the shifts in the 'river-bed' of thoughts (OC 96–97), and could have a truly emancipatory function.

1.4 A Look Ahead

In what follows, we won't consider the *pars destruens* of Wittgenstein's considerations further. Rather, we will focus on his positive views concerning key issues in present-day social epistemology, in the dual sense of anti-individualistic and

9 'How could I shew them that – as I should say – you don't really buy more wood if you buy a pile covering a bigger area? – I should, for instance, take a pile which was small by their ideas and, by laying the logs around, change it into a "big" one. This might convince them – but perhaps they would say: "Yes, now it's a lot of wood and costs more" – and that would be the end of the matter. – We should presumably say in this case: they simply do not mean the same by "a lot of wood" and "a little wood" as we do; and they have a quite different system of payment from us'. I have discussed this passage at length in Coliva (2010: chapter 5) in relation to Wittgenstein's alleged endorsement of thorough-going relativism.

critical social philosophy. First, we will look at Wittgenstein's take on the nature of this shared and inherited background, for which some of his predecessors like Thomas Reid, or even contemporaries like G. E. Moore and Susan Stebbing, reserved the label of 'common sense', and which some theorists today consider 'common knowledge' (Section 2). Then, we will look at Wittgenstein's ground-breaking account of trust in the transmission of hinges (Section 3). Afterwards, we will consider the bearing of Wittgenstein's reflections on so-called 'deep disagreements' – that is, disagreements over hinges (roughly) – which cannot therefore be resolved by applying shared epistemic methods (Section 4). We will connect the treatment of deep disagreement with the question of when the genealogical challenge to the good standing of our beliefs is epistemically significant. Finally, we will look at how Wittgenstein's account of family resemblance in the *Philosophical Investigations*, his views about the authority of avowals, and his remarks on hinges like 'I am a man/woman' may be taken to bear on (i) present-day debates about the concept WOMAN, (ii) the role of self-identification in the determination of one's gender, and (iii) testimonial and hermeneutical injustice (Section 5).

2 Common Sense, Hinges, and Common Knowledge

> The truths which Moore says he knows, are such as, roughly speaking, all of us know, if he knows them
>
> (OC 100)

2.1 Moore (and Newman) on Common Sense

Wittgenstein developed many of the ideas presented in *On Certainty* in response to G. E. Moore's account of common sense. It is therefore apposite to revisit Moore's views before addressing Wittgenstein's. Since 'A defence of common sense' (1925), Moore had held the view that there are several truisms, that is, propositions that are true, and known with certainty to any adult human being, thus constituting a common – that is, shared – body of knowledge. Here is a sample of them (Moore 1925: 33–34):

> There exists at present a living human body, which is my body. This body was born at a certain time in the past, and has existed continuously ever since, though not without undergoing changes . . . Ever since it was born, it has been either in contact with or not far from the surface of the earth; and, at every moment since it was born, there have also existed many other things, having shape and size in three dimensions . . ., from which it has been at various distances . . .; also there have . . . existed some other things of this kind with which it was in contact . . . Among the things which have, in this sense, formed part of its environment . . . there have, at every moment since its birth,

> been large numbers of other living human bodies, each of which has, like it, (a) at some time been born, (b) continued to exist from some time after birth, (c) been, at every moment of its life after birth, either in contact with or not far from the surface of the earth; and many of these bodies have already died and ceased to exist. But the earth had existed also for many years before my body was born; and for many of these years, also, large numbers of human bodies had, at every moment, been alive upon it; and many of these bodies had died and ceased to exist before it was born. Finally (to come to a different class of propositions), I am a human being, and I have, at different times since my body was born, had many different experiences, of each of many different kinds . . . And, just as my body has been the body of a human being, namely myself, who has, during his lifetime, had many experiences of each of these (and other) different kinds; so, in the case of very many of the other human bodies which have lived upon the earth, each has been the body of a different human being, who has, during the lifetime of that body, had many different experiences of each of these (and other) different kinds.

According to Moore (1925: 34), moreover,

> In the case of very many (I do not say all) of the human beings belonging to the class (which includes myself) defined in the following way, i.e. as human beings who have had human bodies, that were born and lived for some time upon the earth, and who have, during the lifetime of those bodies, had many different experiences of each of the kinds mentioned in (1) [the previous list], it is true that each has frequently, during the life of his body, known, with regard to himself or his body, and with regard to some time earlier than any of the times at which I wrote down the propositions in (1), a proposition corresponding to each of the propositions in (1), in the sense that it asserts with regard to himself or his body and the earlier time in question (namely, in each case, the time at which he knew it), just what the corresponding proposition in (1) asserts with regard to me or my body and the time at which I wrote that proposition down.

Moore's truisms were carefully chosen to be as safeguarded from sceptical assaults as possible. They did not include either religious propositions (or presuppositions), contrary to what Thomas Reid (1764) and other philosophers of the Scottish School of Common-Sense Philosophy had maintained,[10] or scientific ones, as Wittgenstein is keen to do in *On Certainty*, as we shall presently see. Nor did Moore focus on the relationship between common sense and science.

[10] For Reid (1764), Nature and humans were created by God, who is perfect and benevolent. Thus, contrary to Hume, on Reid's account there cannot be a clash between the deliverances of reason while doing philosophy, and beliefs formed by means of the exercise of commonsensical judgement, about us, and our place within Nature. James Oswald (1766–1772), another philosopher of the Scottish School of Common-Sense, considers common sense a natural ability to apprehend and judge the truth of certain propositions, including religious ones, which are found to be 'intuitive'.

Contrary to one of his main, unduly forgotten contemporaries – that is, Susan Stebbing[11] – Moore was not exercised by the apparent clash between what Wilfrid Sellars would have called the 'manifest' and the 'scientific image'. Nor was he exercised by the potential clash between common sense and religious dogma. Rather, he thought he could use common sense to oppose *philosophical* theses put forward either by idealist or sceptical philosophers. The former deny the commonsensical truism that there are physical objects and therefore say something false, according to Moore; whereas the latter say something self-contradictory for they claim *we* don't know that there are and have been many human beings besides ourselves, while taking for granted that there are (other) human beings, by talking of what *we* – collectively – don't know.

Furthermore, the groundbreaking role that Moore's defence of common sense has with respect to social epistemology needs to be stressed. For his truisms are indeed the object of common knowledge. That is of knowledge which is possessed by (virtually) all members of the epistemic community and is taken for granted in all our epistemic interactions. Moreover, since they are more certain, for Moore, than any principle one might want to appeal to in the attempt to justify them, it turns out that at the foundation of knowledge there are neither self-evident beliefs like the Cartesian cogito, nor beliefs based on individual experience, but, rather, beliefs about physical entities, including our bodies and their surroundings, which are shared by (virtually) all members of the epistemic community. The classic foundationalist image in which the latter beliefs are grounded on the former is thus completely overturned.

Interestingly, moreover, Moore (1925: 43–44) held that:

> It is, indeed, obvious that, in the case of most of them [i.e. his truisms], I do not know them directly: that is to say, I only know them because, in the past, I have known to be true other propositions which were evidence for them. If, for instance, I do know that the earth had existed for many years before I was born, I certainly only know this because I have known other things in the past which were evidence for it. And I certainly do not know exactly what the evidence was. Yet all this seems to me to be no good reason for doubting that I do know it. We are all, I think, in this strange position that we do know many things, with regard to which we know further that we must have had evidence for them, and yet we do not know how we know them, i.e. we do not know what the evidence was.

Thus, for Moore, truisms are known on the basis of some other proposition, or evidence more generally. Yet, we don't know – that is, we don't recall – what

[11] Stebbing (1937) defends the common-sense view of the world from the attacks launched against it by idealistic interpretations of scientific developments of the time offered by prominent physicists.

that evidence was. However, even if we don't know *how* we know them, we *do know* them nonetheless and indeed know them with certainty, according to him.[12] Needless to say, this confers a weird epistemic status on common sense, especially because it doesn't seem far-fetched to provide some evidence on the basis of which we know, for instance, that we are embodied or that we have lived on or in close proximity to the Earth throughout our lives, or that the Earth has existed long before our birth.

Despite an altogether different account of the scope, epistemic status, and role of common-sense truisms, as we shall see, Wittgenstein concurs with Moore that these truisms play a peculiar role within our epistemic practices and that they are safeguarded against assaults launched by both idealists as well as sceptics.

Before turning to Wittgenstein's account, it is worth mentioning that in the opening passage of *On Certainty*, and in relation to the peculiar epistemic status of the premise of Moore's (1939) celebrated 'Proof of an external world' – that is, 'Here is a hand' – Wittgenstein mentions Cardinal John Henry Newman. As he writes (OC 1):

> If you do know that *here is one hand*, we'll grant you all the rest. When one says that such and such a proposition can't be proved, of course that does not mean that it can't be derived from other propositions; any proposition can be derived from other ones. But they may be no more certain than it is itself. (On this a curious remark by H. Newman.)

Newman, a Catholic theologian, who had converted from Anglicanism and who had become the first rector of the Catholic University of Ireland (now University College Dublin), in his influential *An Essay in Aid of the Grammar of Assent* (1870: 140), had maintained that:

> We are sure beyond all hazard of a mistake, that our own self is not the only being existing; that there is an external world; that it is a system with parts and a whole, a universe carried on by laws; and that the future is affected by the past. We accept and hold with an unqualified assent, that the earth . . . is a globe; that all its regions see the sun by turns; that there are vast tracts on it of land and water; and that there are really existing cities on definite sites, which go by the names of London, Paris, Florence, and Madrid . . . We laugh to scorn the idea that we had no parents, though we have no memory of our birth; that we shall never depart this life, though we can have no experience of the future; that we are able to live without food, though we have never tried; that a world of men did not live before our time, or that that world has had no history.

[12] For a discussion of what I take to be Moore's proto-externalism with respect to knowledge, see Coliva (2010: chapter 1, and 2018 and 2024a). Stebbing (1932) also thought that common-sense truisms are known, and that philosophical arguments meant to either prove or confute them would rest on premises that are less secure than they are.

According to Newman, these propositions which resemble, if only in part, Moore's truisms, are the object of our *assent*. This is a mode of *rational* acceptance, for Newman, of a proposition which is not based on proof, or on conclusive empirical evidence. Writes Newman (1870: 141):

> Assent on reasonings not demonstrative is too widely recognized an act to be irrational, unless man's nature is irrational, too familiar to the prudent and clear-minded to be an infirmity or an extravagance . . . If our nature has any constitution, any laws, one of them is the absolute reception of propositions as true, which lie outside the narrow range of conclusions to which logic, formal or virtual, is tethered.

In fact, the assent is produced by the *illative sense*,[13] according to Newman, which is a faculty or capacity of the rational mind, to produce wholehearted assent to a proposition, even in the absence of proof or conclusive evidence. Writes Newman (1870: 274): 'It is the mind that reasons, and that controls its own reasonings, not any technical apparatus of words and propositions. This power of judging and concluding, when in its perfection, I call the Illative Sense'.

Notice that like Moore, Newman too stresses our inability to mention all our evidence in favour of these propositions, and he too thinks that it would be inconclusive. Still, we have no reason to doubt them, for, as one may put it, borrowing from Wittgenstein, 'nothing in [our] picture of the world speaks in favour of the opposite' (OC 103), and we are therefore rationally entitled to hold on to them. For instance, in connection with our belief that Great Britain is circumnavigable, Newman writes (1870: 294):

> Our reasons for believing that we are circumnavigable are such as these: – first, we have been so taught in our childhood, and it is so in all the maps; next we have never heard it contradicted or questioned; on the contrary, every one whom we have heard speak on the subject of Great Britain, every book we have read, invariably took it for granted, our whole natural history, the routine transactions and current events of the country, our social and commercial system, our political relations with foreigners, imply it in one way or another. Numberless facts, or what we consider facts, rest on the truth of it; no received fact rests on its being otherwise . . . The question is, Why do I believe it myself? . . . I am not insinuating that we are not rational in our certitude; I only mean that we cannot analyse a proof satisfactorily, the result of which good sense actually guarantees to us.

[13] On the nature of the illative sense, see Coliva (2025d). It clearly bears similarities with common sense intended as a peculiar faculty of judgement, like in some members of the Scottish School of Common-Sense philosophy. Cf. fn. 10. The illative sense is responsible for producing assent to a proposition, often supported inferentially, yet not conclusively proved.

Thus, the illative sense manifests itself in acts of virtuous, prudent judgement, which proceed independently of any formal proof or conclusive evidence. Newman likens it to Aristotle's *phronesis* (1870: 275). As he explains in a letter to W. Froude, 'the illative sense is a faculty of the mind which, when properly nurtured, corresponds to Aristotle's *phronesis*. Its field of action isn't virtue but the *inquisitio veri*. This faculty decides for us ... when and how to pass from inference to assent'.[14]

It merits note that, for Newman, the assent produced by the illative sense concerns not only everyday propositions like the ones mentioned in the previously quoted passage, but also religious ones. He thus puts forward a *parity argument* which is meant to vindicate the idea that just as there are many everyday propositions we rationally assent to, even without proof or conclusive evidence, so the assent to religious ones is likewise rational, even though we have no proof, or conclusive evidence of them.[15]

Finally, it must be stressed that while the illative sense is a faculty of the human mind, its proper functioning and flourishing is due to the upbringing within a community of knowers (or believers, in the religious case), which imparts a 'picture of the world' through examples, testimony, and education, as we saw in the previously quoted passage. Consequently, one could assent to propositions one did not assent to previously, or that are not assented to by another person (Newman 1870: chapters 9–10). In other words, the propositions assented to by means of the illative sense far exceed Moore's truisms and are subject to personal and cultural variation. They include religious propositions, as well as broadly scientific ones (e.g., geographical and astronomical truths). Their variety, as we shall see, is thus similar to the multiplicity of 'hinge propositions' we find in *On Certainty*, even though Wittgenstein, at least in that work, does not address religious propositions, and focuses mostly on everyday ones, instead. Contrary to Newman, however, he doesn't presuppose that our assent to them is the outcome of the operations of a peculiar faculty of the rational mind, such as the illative sense. Rather, as we shall see, he claims that we inherit them through our upbringing within an epistemic community that holds them fast, and passes them on to its members, through examples, testimony and education.

2.2 Wittgenstein: Common-Sense Truisms as Hinges

As we saw in the previous section, Wittgenstein thinks that justification, knowledge, and rationally motivated doubts are possible only by taking for

[14] Quoted in Obertello (2000: 97). My translation.

[15] Interpretations of the epistemic status of the propositions which constitute the object of the parity argument diverge among Wittgenstein scholars.

granted a myriad of propositions, which, like hinges, need to stay put if we want the door to turn (OC 341–343).

Their range is wide and includes Moore's truisms, and premises of his proof, Newman's examples (or very similar ones), 'Nobody has ever been to the Moon' (at the time when Wittgenstein was writing, OC 106, 108, 171, 286), 'Water boils at 100 °C' (OC 292, 567, 599, 604), 'Cats don't grow on trees' (OC 282), 'My name is LW' (OC 328, 425), and so on.

Moreover, we also saw that Wittgenstein doesn't think all hinges are on par: some are part of the bedrock, and aren't subject to change, whereas other ones are open to change from context to context or over time. For instance, 'I have two hands' may be a hinge in a Moore-like scenario, while ceasing to be one after a car accident. By contrast, 'There are physical objects' or 'the Earth has existed for a very long time' aren't subject to change.

In *On Certainty* we can discern three main theses regarding hinges,

(1) Hinges aren't empirical propositions;
(2) Hinges aren't known/justified;
(3) Hinges are part of a world-picture.

We will illustrate them in turn. Yet, before embarking on that task, let me clarify that here I am presupposing my own (along several others') interpretation of Wittgenstein's use of the term '*Satz*' as 'proposition'. Contrary to Danièle Moyal-Sharrock's interpretation (2004), and in agreement with Crispin Wright (1985, 2004), Michael Williams (2004), Duncan Pritchard (2015), and as already amply discussed in Coliva (2010, 2013a, b), it must be noted that by the time of *On Certainty* (and already in the *Philosophical Investigations*), Wittgenstein had a family-resemblance conception of propositions.[16] In particular, he had given up on bipolarity – that is, the *possibility* of being *both* true *and* false – as the distinctive feature of genuine propositions.[17] Bipolarity remains the distinctive feature of *empirical* propositions, but propositions extend beyond that domain, to comprise, in *On Certainty*, those hinges which, while having a descriptive content, do not play an empirical role, for they are not open to empirical investigation, either because they are presupposed by all investigations, or else because the investigation is closed with respect to them. In this sense, their role is more like that of rules, rather than of empirical propositions (OC 95–96). Furthermore, some of them are mostly implicit and

[16] OC 320, cf. OC 318–319, and PI 65, for criticism of the Tractarian idea of 'the general form of the proposition'.

[17] Bipolarity, therefore, isn't bivalence. For Wittgenstein, bivalence holds only when we need to determine whether a proposition is *actually* true *or* false. In the case of empirical propositions, we proceed to that determination by means of an empirical inquiry.

are hardly ever expressed – for example 'There are physical objects' or 'I have hands' – whereas some of them are acquired through testimony from other members of our linguistic community – for example 'Water boils at 100 °C', or 'Nobody has ever been on the Moon' (at the time). Whereas the former is manifested mostly in our actions and in our ways of thinking and inferring, and yet, if one had the relevant concepts, could be expressed if requested, the latter are explicitly taught, even though, once acquired, they are taken for granted without being subject to any further investigation.

2.2.1 Hinges Aren't Empirical Propositions

As we saw in Section 1, hinges are propositions about material objects, which, however, do not play a genuinely empirical role (OC 401–402). For, contrary to genuinely empirical propositions, they are not open to investigation. Rather, they stay put, and play the role of rules (OC 94–95, 98, 308–309), meaning that they do not need to give way to alleged counterevidence. Just as we don't revise '2 + 2 = 4' if, after buying two apples and two oranges, we find only three pieces of fruit in our bag, similarly, we don't typically revise any of the propositions that play a hinge role. If we do so, it is only after demoting them to the role of genuinely empirical propositions and after subjecting them to empirical investigation. Furthermore, at least some hinges function as norms of evidential significance. That is, by staying put, they allow certain kinds of evidence to be used to justify other, genuinely empirical propositions. For instance, it is only by taking for granted that there are physical objects that we can take our sensory experience to bear onto beliefs about specific physical objects around us; and it is only by taking for granted that the Earth has existed for a long time that we can take (what appear to be) fossils to bear on the determination of its age, say. In this case, hinges allow us to surpass our 'cognitive locality' so that propositions about mind-*independent* objects can be justified by means of mind-*dependent* experiences; or propositions about the distant unobserved/able past can be justified by means of observable data. Similarly, if we started repeatedly forgetting our name, we would start losing confidence in our memory to determine other issues, for example, where we parked our car in the parking lot. Likewise, if we couldn't see the hand we hold in front of us, we could no longer rely on our eyesight to determine what other objects there are in our immediate surroundings, and so on. Undoubtedly, there is a difference among these cases, for remembering one's name doesn't seem key to rational inquiry in the same way as taking for granted the existence of physical objects. However, not remembering one's name would be a *symptom* of the malfunctioning of our memory; likewise, not seeing or feeling our hands, would be a symptom of the malfunctioning of our senses (including proprioception). Thus, we could no longer confidently rely on these important sources of justification and knowledge for many of our ordinary inquiries and would start looking for the physical and/or psychological causes of the malfunctioning.

The idea that hinges function as norms, at least in context, is at the root of those passages in which Wittgenstein denies that they are subject to semantic evaluation and states that they are therefore neither true nor false. Here is a characteristic sample (OC 94–95):

> But I did not get my picture of the world by satisfying myself of its correctness: nor do I have it because I am satisfied of its correctness. No: it is the inherited background against which I distinguish between true and false.
>
> The propositions describing this world-picture might be part of a kind of mythology. And their role is like that of rules of a game; and the game can be learned purely practically, without learning any explicit rules.

Or at least, hinges aren't true either because they correspond to a mind-independent reality of facts that makes them true, or because they are maximally supported by our evidence.[18] For we need to presuppose the existence of a world constituted by mind-independent objects to make sense of a correspondence-theoretic account of truth for ordinary empirical propositions. Thus, 'There are physical objects' cannot itself be a relatum in a T-schema such as

(T) < There are physical objects > is true iff there are physical objects,

and can only be the presupposition upon on which specific instances of the T-schema may so much as be formulated. That is, since PHYSICAL OBJECT is a 'logical concept' (OC 36) like COLOUR and QUANTITY rather than a genuine concept, we cannot affirm its existence, for Wittgenstein (OC 35–37).[19]

Moreover, according to him, if one thought that 'if everything speaks for a hypothesis and nothing against it' (OC 191) it certainly 'agrees with reality [that is, with mind-independent] facts', one would already be 'going round in a circle' (OC 191, cf. 203). For 'agreeing with reality' means, in Wittgenstein's thought after the *Tractatus*, that everything speaks for a proposition and nothing against it. Again, according to him, 'the reason why the use of the expression "true or false" has something misleading about it is that it is like saying "it tallies with the facts or it doesn't", and the very thing that is in question is what 'tallying' is here.' (OC 199). For there can be a 'tallying' with a mind-independent reality, only if we take for granted there are physical – that is, mind-independent – objects.

[18] Williams (2004) suggested that we are to think of hinges as minimally true. See Wright (1992) for a minimalist account of truth.

[19] See also Section 4.5.

Furthermore, hinges make it possible to acquire empirical evidence and to raise rationally motivated doubts about specific objects and states of affairs. Given their role, then, nothing can speak against them. For local doubts would have to presuppose them and global ones would be meaningless and not rational, for Wittgenstein (see Section 1.2). However, the fact that nothing can speak against them and that everything speaks in their favour does not mean that they are true because they are maximally justified by the evidence at our disposal. For they make it possible for that evidence to play a justificatory role in the first place. Thus, neither a correspondentist nor an epistemic conception of truth applies to hinges. Rather, hinges determine the conditions of possibility for saying that a given proposition *p* tallies with the facts and is therefore true; as well as for saying that *p* is true because all our evidence speaks in favour of it.

Finally, it merits note that for Wittgenstein (OC 96, 210)

> It might be imagined that some propositions, of the form of empirical propositions, were hardened and functioned as channels for such empirical propositions as were not hardened but fluid; and that this relation altered with time, in that fluid propositions hardened, and hard ones became fluid.
>
> Does my telephone call to New York strengthen my conviction that the earth exists? Much seems to be fixed, and it is removed from the traffic. It is so to speak shunted onto an unused siding.

The idea, then, is that at least in some cases, hinges may start out as ordinary empirical propositions. Yet, when there is so much evidence in their favour that inquiry about them is closed and they start being taken for granted within an epistemic practice, they turn into hinges. That is, they are no longer subject to semantic evaluation and are protected against doubts and (alleged) counter-evidence. In this sense, therefore, their role changes from genuinely empirical to rule-like. Wittgenstein writes the following (OC 162–163):

> In general I take as true what is found in text-books, of geography for example. Why? I say: All these facts have been confirmed a hundred times over. But how do I know that? What is my evidence for it? I have a world-picture. Is it true or false? Above all it is the substratum of all my enquiring and asserting. The propositions describing it are not all equally subject to testing.

To repeat, just like we do not doubt that ‘2 + 2 = 4’ even if after buying two apples and two oranges we go home and find we only have three pieces of fruit, we don’t doubt that we have hands, that our name is thus-and-so, that the Earth has existed for a long time, and that it isn’t flat, even if on occasion we might not see or feel them, or someone might suggest that we are named otherwise, or that the Earth is flat. Still, on occasion, at least some of them may go back to their empirical role. For instance, after a car accident one can legitimately investigate if one still has hands; or, after a major discovery about being abducted as a child, one may rightfully wonder what one's real name is, and so on. Likewise, after major technological developments, a once-upon-a-time hinge like 'Nobody has ever been on the Moon' has gone back to being an ordinary empirical proposition, which is now correctly considered to be false.

2.2.2 Hinges Aren't Known/Justified

According to Wittgenstein, hinges are not known or justified. Nor are they open to doubt, for that matter. For doubt is possible only when it is possible to have reasons against a proposition and it is therefore possible not to know it. Rather hinges are altogether beyond epistemic appraisal. This may happen for two different reasons, though, depending on the kind of hinge at hand.

First, it may happen because the relevant hinges are presupposed by any (alleged) proof we might want to give of them. This is the case, for instance, with 'There are physical objects', which far from being supported by a Moore-like proof, needs to be presupposed for the proof to start with justified, or known premises. That is, we can justifiably believe/know, based on sensory experience, that there is a hand where we seem to see it, only by taking for granted that there are physical objects, broadly manifest in perception. Thus, we cannot prove that conclusion by starting with that kind of premise.

Second, a hinge may be beyond epistemic appraisal because it is presupposed by the kind of inquiry in sight. For instance, in astronomy, it is nowadays taken for granted that the Earth revolves around the Sun and not vice versa. We inquire and possibly dispute about other things, but that is held fast.

In the former case, then, no (empirical) justification can be acquired for hinges and therefore, if knowledge entails having a justification for one's belief, hinges aren't known.[20] In the latter case, in contrast, in virtue of the overwhelming evidence in favour of a given proposition, inquiry about it is closed; it is no longer possible to rationally doubt the proposition, and it becomes the yardstick by means of which measurement is possible, at least within a given context or at a given time.

Now, it merits note that, as we saw in Section 1, while discussing the use of 'I know' in connection with one's own sensations and intentions, Wittgenstein allows for a 'grammatical' use of it. In OC (58) he writes:

> If "I know etc." is conceived as a grammatical proposition, of course the I cannot be important. And it properly means "There is no such thing as a doubt in this case" or "The expression 'I do not know' makes no sense in this case". And of course it follows from this that "I *know*" makes no sense either.

[20] Or else, if they are known, they are known in the sense of 'animal knowledge', not of 'reflective knowledge'.

'I know' in connection with hinges thus serves a similarly *grammatical* function. In either case, it signals the fact that – for albeit different reasons – there is no doubt or open inquiry with respect to hinges and they are taken for granted, at least in context and at a particular time, in our further inquiries. 'I know' with respect to them therefore expresses the pivotal role the hinge plays in our shared epistemic practices, in which it is taken for granted that besides 'knowing' general facts regarding the long existence of the Earth, or that there are physical objects, people also know their own names or have reliable memories regarding major events in their pasts. Were this not the case, and all else being equal in terms of conceptual mastery and sincerity, we would thereby be entitled to think that there is something wrong with their psychiatric condition.

A recent proposal has been made by John Greco (2016, 2021) according to which hinges are the content of *common knowledge*. Common knowledge, for him, is neither knowledge we acquire by ourselves – either through experience or through reasoning – nor knowledge that we acquire from others, through testimony. Rather, items of common knowledge are freely available to us by being part of an epistemic community. In the 'knowledge economy', therefore, they aren't goods we acquire by ourselves or that we inherit from others, but, like water or air, are freely available to us. Furthermore, Greco thinks they are items of procedural knowledge – that is knowledge that is tacitly presupposed while carrying out actions and several cognitive tasks.

As we saw, however, Wittgenstein thinks of hinges as often if not always inherited from a community, and thus testimony and education – for example, through textbooks, and so on – are essential to hinge acquisition. Furthermore, he isn't opposed to the idea that, at least in some cases, we acquire them through repeated experience and retain them in memory. For instance, we know our name because we have been called this throughout our entire life. Thus, the idea that hinges are the object of a *sui generis* kind of knowledge, which goes beyond experience, memory, and testimony, is alien to *On Certainty*. True, hinges aren't subject to any investigation or quality-check, at least in context, and thus circulate freely within the knowledge economy. Yet, *ab origine*, they are either acquired through usual epistemic methods, or else, like in the case of the existence of physical objects or the long existence of the Earth, are taken for granted without the possibility of being (non-circularly) empirically supported.

Finally, as to Greco's further claim that they are the objects of procedural knowledge, meaning that they are tacitly operative in our acting and thinking and are often embodied or enacted, it may be the case that 'I have hands' or 'My name is AC' get so internalized that they become items of procedural knowledge. Yet, it is difficult to extend this idea to many other hinges Wittgenstein considers, such as that water boils at 100 °C, that nobody had ever been to the Moon, that cats don't grow on trees, and so on.

Thus, if we may talk of common – that is, shared – knowledge in connection with hinges, we should not interpret it as a special, *sui generis* and mysterious kind of knowledge, alternative to knowledge based on experience, reasoning, memory, or testimony. Rather, we should conceive of it as a lack of doubt, not primarily because one has personally verified it or is especially well-positioned to know it, but because what is said – grammatically – to be known plays a constitutive role in our shared epistemic practices.

2.2.3 Hinges Are Part of a World-Picture

Here is how Wittgenstein introduces the idea that hinges are part of a world-picture (OC 93):

> The propositions presenting what Moore '*knows*' are all of such a kind that it is difficult to imagine *why* anyone should believe the contrary. E.g. the proposition that Moore has spent his whole life in close proximity to the earth. – Once more I can speak of myself here instead of speaking of Moore. What could induce me to believe the opposite? Either a memory, or having been told. – Everything that I have seen or heard gives me the conviction that no man has ever been far from the earth. Nothing in my picture of the world speaks in favour of the opposite.

As we have seen multiple times, this picture is inherited (OC 94) from our community and isn't something we form in isolation. It is a background (OC 94) against which we judge and therefore engage in semantic and epistemic evaluations, and not something the correctness of which we have personally tested. For, as we will see at length in the next section, all testing already presupposes hinges.

It merits note that, for Wittgenstein, it is a picture (OC 93–95, 167, 233, 262), an image (OC 146–147), which guides our actions and judgements. Yet, it is akin to a mythology. As he writes (OC 95–96):

> The propositions describing this world-picture might be part of a kind of mythology. And their role is like that of rules of a game; and the game can be learned purely practically, without learning any explicit rules.
>
> It might be imagined that some propositions, of the form of empirical propositions, were hardened and functioned as channels for such empirical propositions as were not hardened but fluid; and that this relation altered with time, in that fluid propositions hardened, and hard ones became fluid.

Thus, hinges, like a mythology, are often acquired merely by taking part in a shared epistemic (compare: a religious) practice, and, as we saw, they may change over time and according to context (OC 97) (compare: we no longer believe in Homer's gods).

Finally, being part of an image, and the background or substratum by means of which we are able to produce reasons, a change of hinges will likely not be based on arguments – for reasons get to an end (OC 110) and at that point 'my spade is turned' (PI 217). Rather, as Wittgenstein puts it, it will be based on *persuasion* (OC 262, cf. 233):

> I can imagine a man who had grown up in quite special circumstances and been taught that the earth came into being 10 years ago, and therefore believed this. We might instruct him: the earth has long . . . etc. – We should be trying to give him our picture of the world. This would happen through a kind of *persuasion*.

In closing, it is worth pointing out that, on this account, it is in the nature of all investigations – empirical, mathematical, and also philosophical – that giving reasons comes to an end and that, at the end, we find the pictures or images that have guided our thinking throughout and that allow reasons to be produced in favour of 'ordinary' propositions in each of these domains. A change in view, in any of these domains, then, eventually rests on getting rid of old pictures and on embracing new ones and will therefore depend on ultimately causal factors. We will investigate the role of causal factors and persuasion in the context of our discussion of deep disagreements in Section 4.

3 Testimony and Trust

> I really want to say that a language-game is only possible if one trusts something (I did not say "can trust something").
>
> (OC 509)

3.1 Wittgenstein on Testimony

Testimony, as we saw, is central to the transmission of hinges and, thus, to the transmission of what needs to stay put for us to be able to acquire justification for, and knowledge of ordinary empirical propositions. As Wittgenstein writes in OC (94):

> I did not get my picture of the world by satisfying myself of its correctness; nor do I have it because I am satisfied of its correctness. No: it is the inherited background against which I distinguish between true and false.

Testimony relevant to the transmission of hinges takes place not only through direct interactions between human beings, in various situations characteristic of human upbringing and education, but also indirectly, by means of textbooks, the media or, today, by means of the internet.

Testimony in general is successful in transmitting justification or knowledge only if the attestor is trustworthy – that is, knowledgeable and sincere with respect to what they are asserting. Testimony is one of the topics in social epistemology which has received the most attention in recent years. For so-called 'reductionists' (who develop the Humean position, like Fricker 1994), testimony manages to transmit justification and knowledge only if one has independent reasons to think that the attestor is trustworthy. By contrast, for 'anti-reductionists' (who develop a Reidian position, like Burge 1993), no such independent reasons are needed. All that is needed is that one has no reason to think that the attestor is untrustworthy.

Wittgenstein seems to object to the reductionist viewpoint. We don't seem to need to ascertain the epistemic credentials of attestors before being able to acquire justified beliefs and knowledge from them. As Wittgenstein writes in OC (23):

> If I don't know whether someone has two hands (say, whether they have been amputated or not) I shall believe his assurance that he has two hands, if he is trustworthy. And if he says he *knows* it, that can only signify to me that he has been able to make sure, and hence that his arms are e.g. not still concealed by coverings and bandages, etc. etc. My believing the trustworthy man stems from my admitting that it is possible for him to make sure.

That is, if the attestor is trustworthy – that is, knowledgeable and sincere with respect to what they are saying – then we do acquire knowledge (or at least justified belief) from them without having to ascertain their epistemic credentials.[21]

Still, in the case of hinges, according to Wittgenstein, it isn't because they have been passed on to us by trustworthy people that we know or believe them. In fact, as the reader will recall from Sections 1 and 2, hinges aren't known, in the 'empirical' or 'epistemic' sense of 'knowing'. Nor are they believed in the k- or j-apt sense of 'believing'. At most, they are known in the grammatical sense of 'knowing' which, as we saw in the previous section, may be glossed as 'it stands fast for me and many others that . . . '. Writes Wittgenstein in OC (137):

> Even if the most trustworthy of men assures me that he *knows* things are thus and so, this by itself cannot satisfy me that he does know. Only that he believes he knows. That is why Moore's assurance that he knows . . . does not interest us. The propositions, however, which Moore retails as examples of such known truths are indeed interesting. Not because anyone knows their

[21] It isn't clear, though, whether Wittgenstein opts for an anti-reductionist account. Some hints in that direction can be found in RPP II, §§602-3. In my own development of hinge epistemology, I have proposed a hinge-account of testimonial justification, which steers a middle path between reductionism and anti-reductionism. See Coliva (2019).

> truth, or believes he knows them, but because they all have a *similar* role in the system of our empirical judgments.

Furthermore, it is only by possessing a language and the hinges characteristic of our various epistemic practices that we can then go on to form reasons, on specific occasions, to doubt or ascertain the trustworthiness of attestors. Thus, any judgement regarding attestors' trustworthiness – that is, their being knowledgeable and sincere – depends on already possessing the hinges necessary for such a determination. As such, it cannot be the case that one must first judge that the attestor is trustworthy before one can acquire a hinge from them (see also Hertzberg (1988) and Lagerspetz (1998: 94) on this point). This, by itself, is of course compatible with both the reductionist and anti-reductionist positions concerning genuine transmissions of knowledge (or justification) in the case of ordinary beliefs. Yet, we have seen some reasons to think that Wittgenstein was not inclined towards reductionism on that front either.

3.2 Wittgenstein on Trust and Hinges

Still, for Wittgenstein, trust is crucial to the transmission of hinges. In fact, out of the 676 entries in *On Certainty*, approximately thirty are devoted to this topic.[22] This is due to the fact that he decouples trust from trustworthiness. For he rightly divorces the issue of what trust is from the issue of when it is merited, and hence from the issue of under which conditions someone is worthy of trust, which may indeed vary according to context. For instance, being a trustworthy attestor amounts to being sincere and knowledgeable, as we have seen, whereas being a trustworthy spouse means to be supportive and faithful (at the very least), and being a trustworthy friend means to be supportive, loyal, and sincere, say. This runs contrary to a whole tradition of thinking of the relationship between trust and trustworthiness which we find already in Hobbes,[23] and revisited in contemporary authors (Hardin 2002, Hawley 2019), who take trustworthiness to be prior to trust, in the analysis of these cognate notions.

Be that as it may, trust has been subject to intense debate over the last few decades, at least since Baier (1986). Much ink has been spilled on whether trust differs from reliance, and if so, which further conditions need to obtain to give rise to trust (call these 'reliance +' accounts).[24]

---

[22] Indirect reference to trust is quite ubiquitous in OC, especially when he talks about 'taking for granted', 'standing fast', 'not-doubting', and 'believing' in a non j/k-apt way.

[23] Hobbes (1640: 44) defines trust as 'A Passion proceeding from the *Belief of him* from whom we *expect* or *hope* for Good, so *free* from *Doubt* that upon the same we pursue no other way to attain the same Good'.

[24] We will consider the bearing of Wittgenstein's proposal on the contemporary debate on trust in Section 3.4.

What Wittgenstein says in this respect in *On Certainty* is refreshing. For he thinks that trust in fact characterizes our relationship to hinges. We trust that there are material objects, that what has regularly happened in the past will keep repeating in the future, that the Earth has existed for a very long time, that we have hands and that we have never been too far away from the surface of the Earth (individually or at least as mankind up to the late 1960s). Furthermore, he thinks that we trust people (experts and non-experts alike), but also memory, our sensory faculties, objects, and artefacts (such as textbooks, or as we might think today, the internet), even if we don't know how they operate, who has created or designed them, and so on. Thus, he goes beyond the dichotomy between trust and reliance we find in much of the contemporary literature.[25] Moreover, he does not propose sets of necessary and jointly sufficient conditions for trust. Rather, he characterizes it as a basic stance of openness and reliance with respect to others, but also with respect to objects and artefacts, as well as our own faculties.

In more detail: for Wittgenstein, trust is manifested not only towards people, but also towards our faculties, like our senses and our memory. As he writes in OC (34, 337. Cf. 125, 133):

> If someone is taught to calculate, is he also taught that he can rely on a calculation of his teacher's? But these explanations must after all sometime come to an end. Will he also be taught that he can **trust his senses** – since he is indeed told in many cases that in such and such a special case you *cannot* **trust them**? – Rule and exception.
>
> When I write a letter and post it, I take it for granted that it will arrive – I expect this. If I make an experiment I do not doubt the existence of the apparatus before my eyes. I have plenty of doubts, but not *that*. If I do a calculation I believe, without any doubts, that the figures on the paper aren't switching of their own accord, and I also **trust my memory** the whole time, and **trust it without any reservation**. The certainty here is the same as that of my never having been on the moon.

Moreover, according to him, we trust textbooks, even if we have only a rough idea of how the latter are produced,[26] and we trust epistemic authorities. As he writes in OC (599, 600, and 604):

> For example one could describe the certainty of the proposition that water boils at *circa* 100 °C. That isn't e.g. a proposition I have once heard (like this or that, which I could mention). I made the experiment myself at school. The proposition is a very elementary one in our **text-books**, which **are to be trusted** in matters like this because . . .

[25] *Contra* Hertzberg 1988, who, however, points out that he isn't engaging in exegesis (1988: 308).

[26] Compare trusting Google and Google maps in our everyday lives with generally having a very rough idea of how they work.

> What kind of grounds have I for **trusting text-books** of experimental physics? **I have no grounds for not trusting them. And I trust them**. I know how such books are produced – or rather, I believe I know. I have some evidence, but it does not go very far and is of a very scattered nature. I have heard, seen and read various things.
>
> In a court of law the statement of a physicist that water boils at about 100 °C would be accepted unconditionally as truth. **If I mistrusted this statement what could I do to undermine it? Set up experiments myself? What would they prove**?

Once again, we do not trust our senses, memory, textbooks, or epistemic authorities because they have proved trustworthy or because we deem them so. Rather, we trust them and that allows us to acquire certain hinges from each of them. Our attitude of trust towards these sources carries over to the hinges we acquire from them. Only once in possession of such hinges, can we assess the trustworthiness of these sources and, from time to time, the good standing of (at least some) hinges as well.[27]

Thus, trust is transcendentally prior to trustworthiness as well as to distrust or even the mere lack of trust,[28] for a judgement of trustworthiness depends on having ascertained whether a speaker, for instance, is knowledgeable and sincere. Yet, to ascertain that much, we need a language and epistemic methods, with their attendant hinges, which we have, in their turn, only thanks to trusting people, objects, our faculties, and so on. Trust, therefore, is transcendentally prior to trustworthiness, as well as to distrust, which can ensue only when there are good reasons to think that a speaker is, say, ignorant or insincere (or perhaps both). Yet trust is also prior to the suspension of judgement with respect to whether someone is trustworthy or indeed untrustworthy, and indeed prior to the mere absence of trust, from an epistemic point of view. For we need to accept what we are told in order to acquire the language and hinges necessary for obtaining and deploying the epistemic methods which would allow us legitimately to consider someone as trustworthy or untrustworthy – thus overcoming the absence of trust – or to reflectively suspend judgement about the issue. As Wittgenstein writes in OC (150–151, 509. Cf. 301–308)

> How do I know that this colour is blue? If I don't **trust** *myself* here, why should I **trust anyone else's judgment**? Is there a why? **Must I not begin to trust somewhere**? That is to say: somewhere **I must begin with not-doubting; and that is not, so to speak, hasty but excusable: it is part of judging**. (OC 150)

---

27 This is key if, as Wittgenstein holds, hinges may change over time. Trust is therefore a stance we have towards objects, people, our faculties, etc. and is thus 'objectual'. Yet, thanks to it, we acquire hinges that have propositional content and are constitutive of our epistemic practices.

28 It is customary in the literature on trust to distinguish between trust, lack of trust and distrust.

> I should like to say: Moore does not *know* what he asserts he knows, but it stands fast for him, as also for me; regarding it as absolutely solid is part of our *method* of doubt and enquiry. (OC 151)

> I really want to say that a language-game is only **possible if one trusts something (I did not say "can trust something")**. (OC 509)

And famously, in the very passages where the metaphor of hinges is introduced (OC 341–343), he writes:

> That is to say, the *questions* that we raise and our *doubts* depend on the fact that some propositions are exempt from doubt, are as it were like hinges on which those turn.
>
> That is to say, it belongs to the logic of our scientific investigations that certain things are *in deed* not doubted.
>
> But it isn't that the situation is like this: We just *can't* investigate everything, and for that reason we are forced to rest content with assumption. If I want the door to turn, the hinges must stay put.

Thus, it is part of the logic – that is the norms – of scientific investigation (and of any other kind of empirical investigation) for Wittgenstein, that certain propositions are *in deed* not doubted and are therefore *taken on trust* (OC 159).

Furthermore, trust is psychologically prior to distrust for Wittgenstein. For, as children (OC 159–162) we first trust, then only later, after having acquired a language and various epistemic methods, do we proceed to form reasons to distrust (or to suspend judgement, say, or indeed to form a judgement about someone's trustworthiness). (Cf. Stern 2017 and Moyal-Sharrock 2005: chapter 9). As Wittgenstein writes in OC (159–162):

> As children we learn facts; e.g. that every human being has a brain, and *we take them on trust*. I believe that there is an island, Australia, of such-and-such a shape, and so on and so on; I believe that I had great-grandparents, that the people who gave themselves out as my parents really were my parents, etc. This belief may never have been expressed; even the thought that it was so, never thought.
>
> The child learns by believing the adult. **Doubt comes *after* belief.**[29]
>
> I learned an enormous amount and **accepted it on human authority**, and then I found some things confirmed or disconfirmed by my own experience.
>
> In general I take as true what is found in text-books, of geography for example. Why? I say: All these facts have been confirmed a hundred times

[29] Recall that this is the sense of 'belief' that is not k- or j-apt. Wittgenstein also maintains (CE, 383) that adults believe children, in this sense, for instance when they instinctively express pain, or other feelings and emotions. If they didn't, their behaviour would not be considered prudent but insensitive or pathological.

> over. But how do I know that? What is my evidence for it? I have a **world-picture**. Is it true or false? Above all it is the **substratum of all my enquiring and asserting**. The propositions describing it are not all equally subject to testing.

As a stance, hinge trust is also part of our psychologically inbuilt way of approaching reality.[30] That is, as children we tend to trust adults and various authorities, as well as certain worldly regularities. Our doing so – with no grounds or reasons in their favour, at that point – is crucial to the acquisition of language and methods of inquiry, with their own respective hinges, which make it possible to then go on investigating the epistemic credentials of our initial trust, if need be, both with respect to the source of the information and about the information itself.

In addition, for Wittgenstein, evidence can be the cause of and/or can keep corroborating our trust in hinges, but it cannot epistemically ground it, for all our evidence depends on taking hinges for granted (OC 275–280), either contextually, or globally. As he writes in OC (429),

> What reason have I, now, when I cannot see my toes, to assume that I have five toes on each foot? Is it right to say that my reason is that previous experience has always taught me so? Am I more certain of previous experience than that I have ten toes? That previous experience may very well be the *cause* of my present certitude; but is it its **ground**?

This connects with what we saw in Section 2. It may be that having seen or felt our toes a myriad of times it becomes a hinge for us and thus something which is no longer in need of evidential support but rather stands fast for us and against which we measure our sight or proprioception. Once turned into a hinge, however, evidence putatively in favour of such a proposition either presupposes it or is no more secure than the very hinge it should epistemically support. Conversely, the fact that evidence cannot speak against a hinge should not be taken to epistemically support it either. For it is in the very nature of hinges that, once understood as norms, evidence putatively against them is either discounted or explained away.

The best way of characterizing hinge trust, therefore, is as a basic stance of openness and reliance (OC 201–213, 508–509, 514–515, 571) on something and/or someone. It is a stance because it comes *before and independently of* being able to have j/k-apt beliefs. It is a stance of openness meaning that, when we occupy it, we act and take in information without questioning either its source or its content. In this sense, it is an *unquestioning* attitude we have towards what we trust. It is a stance of reliance – that is, of *dependence* – on objects, people, cognitive faculties, and/or institutional practices to provide us

[30] *Contra* Hertzberg (1988: 316), but recall that he claims he is not engaging in exegesis.

with language, methods of inquiry, and other epistemic capacities we need to form judgements and beliefs. As we saw, moreover, it is a basic psychological stance we have as part of our psychological make-up, which serves us well. For, to repeat, it is needed to acquire anything relevant to the entertaining of propositional contents and to their epistemic assessment.[31]

Notice that even if hinge trust can be characterized as a form of reliance, this does not mean endorsing a reliabilist account of it. For, according to Wittgenstein, it is not because certain sources of information and methods are conducive to the formation of true beliefs that we trust them (or that our trust in them is justified, or otherwise in epistemically good standing). Rather, we act in a certain way – that is, we do trust our senses, memory, textbooks, experts, and so on. That gives us a certain picture of the world – that is, a set of hinges (OC 93–97, 162, 167, 262). Based on that, we then distinguish between what is true or false, justified or unjustified, known or unknown (OC 94). Thus, it is only by trusting *first* that we can acquire the means to, *then*, form and evaluate beliefs and their sources as reliable or unreliable. As he writes in OC (508–509, 514–515):

> What can I rely on?
>
> I really want to say that a language-game is only possible if one trusts something (I did not say "can trust something").
>
> This statement appeared to me fundamental; if it is false, what are 'true' and 'false' any more?!
>
> If my name is not L.W., how can I rely on what is meant by "true" and "false"?

And he continues in OC (94, 205):

> But I did not get my picture of the world by satisfying myself of its correctness; nor do I have it because I am satisfied of its correctness. No: **it is the inherited background against which I distinguish between true and false**.
>
> If the true is what is grounded, then the ground is not true, not yet false.

Hinge trust, moreover, has a distinctive phenomenology, characterized by feeling secure and certain. That is, 'The reasonable man does not have certain doubts' (OC 220). Hinges too, in many cases at least, are something we feel

[31] On this reading, trust is basic and characterizes our relationship to hinges. Understood in this way, the view doesn't seem open to any of the objections Pritchard (2023) presents, objections which largely depend on working with a notion of trust that is at odds with Wittgenstein's. For hinge trust, contrary to Pritchard's notion of trust, is in fact incompatible with doubt or open-mindedness or agnosticism. Moreover, Pritchard's claim that trust can be revoked, while our endorsement of hinges cannot and thus should not be seen as trust, is unconvincing. Hinges, after all, can and do change. Additionally, one could argue that the irrevocability of hinge trust marks a distinction between it and other forms of trust.

certain and secure about, for example, we feel certain and secure about our name, or about having hands, or about being born on a certain date in a given place. Yet, it is not this feeling that makes a hinge certain and secure. What makes a hinge certain is the role that hinge we basically trust/rely upon plays in the system of our judgement: it allows us to acquire evidence and justification for, and therefore knowledge of, ordinary empirical propositions, but also the means to doubt and inquire into ordinary empirical propositions.

Furthermore, hinge trust – in the dual sense of a basic attitude of openness and reliance, as well as of an attitude we most fundamentally have towards hinges – normally goes unspoken, and for this reason, it is almost 'invisible' and in a sense 'elusive'. We take it for granted and it normally goes without saying that there are physical objects, or that the Earth has existed for a very long time, that this is my hand, that people know their own names, or that we can rely on our senses and memory (OC 94–95, 103, 397, 500–501, 568). Here is Wittgenstein (OC 95, 397, 568, 103):

> The propositions describing this world-picture might be part of a kind of mythology. And their role is like that of rules of a game; and the game can be learned **purely practically, without learning any explicit rules**.
>
> Haven't I gone wrong and isn't Moore perfectly right? Haven't I made the elementary mistake of confusing one's thoughts with one's knowledge? Of course **I do not think to myself "The earth already existed for some time before my birth"**, but do I *know* it any the less? Don't I show that I know it by always drawing its consequences?
>
> If one of my names were used only very rarely, then it might happen that I did not know it. **It goes without saying** that I know my name, only because, like anyone else, I use it over and over again.
>
> And now if I were to say "It is my unshakeable conviction that etc.", this means in the present case too that **I have not consciously arrived at the conviction** by following a particular line of thought, but that it is anchored in all my *questions and answers*, so anchored that I cannot touch it.

Conversely, trust tends to become phenomenologically salient either when things do not work as expected – whence distrust may ensue – or when we are confronted with something unfamiliar and unexpected; so that what we normally take for granted or what goes without saying can no longer be assumed. Interestingly, raising doubts about hinges or indeed affirming that one knows them, when that is normally taken for granted, raises the issue of the legitimacy of our trust in them to the point of possibly annihilating it, at least within the philosophy seminar. Here is Wittgenstein again (OC 423, 481, 500–501)

> Then why don't I simply say with Moore "I *know* that I am in England?" Saying this is meaningful *in particular circumstances*, which I can imagine.

> **But when I utter the sentence outside these circumstances, as an example to show that I can know truths of this kind with certainty, then it at once strikes me as fishy**. – Ought it to?
>
> When one hears Moore say "I *know* that that's a tree", **one suddenly understands those who think that that has by no means been settled. The matter strikes one all at once as being unclear and blurred. It is as if Moore had put it in the wrong light**.
>
> But **it would also strike me as nonsense to say** "I know that the law of induction is true". Imagine such a statement made in a court of law! It would be more correct to say "I believe in the law of . . . " where 'believe' has nothing to do with *surmising*.
>
> Am I not getting closer and closer to saying that in the end **logic cannot be described**? You must look at the practice of language, then you will see it.

In sum, our trust in hinges – and trust more generally – is operating in the 'background' of all our thinking, judging, and inquiring. Very rarely does it come to the foreground, and when it does, as it does when we do philosophy, it suddenly appears dubious. Of course, for Wittgenstein philosophy cannot overturn our basic certainties, but, for sure, raising the issue of the rational legitimacy of our trust in hinges as we do in the philosophy seminar does have the effect of making us uncertain about it and its content. This phenomenological point – as disturbing as it might be – is however entirely consistent with then finding, within the philosophy seminar, reasons to resist such an outcome. Indeed, *On Certainty* can be seen as aiming just at that (see Moyal-Sharrock 2005 and Coliva 2010 for a reconstruction of Wittgenstein's anti-sceptical strategies). Moore's and Stebbing's philosophies of common sense may be seen as aiming at the same target, as we saw in Section 2.[32] That is, they too would insist that basic trust in Moore's truisms and premises of his proof is legitimate as such. That is, philosophy can neither epistemically ground nor overturn it.

What Wittgenstein's account of trust brings to light is the Janus-faced nature of trust. On the one hand, trust is characterized by a phenomenology of feeling secure and at ease both with our human and with our non-human environment. On the other, it is a stance that constitutively opens us up to the possibility of being let down. Far from being a problem, however, this just shows that this form of dependence is in fact a condition of our success as individuals and as a species. In this sense, such an account of trust illuminates what it means to say that humans are a social species. For at the heart of our individual and collective success, there is a reliance on others (as well as on several aspects of our environment) that allows us, as individuals and as a species, to acquire and

[32] See Coliva (2010 and 2021a) for a discussion of Moore's and Stebbing's positions respectively.

transmit all necessary elements for forming beliefs and assessing them. To repeat, we do not trust because it has proved successful. Rather, we trust and that is what enables us to be successful – it allows us to possess a language and methods of inquiry that can vastly extend our knowledge and then it allows us to pass such knowledge (including linguistic knowledge) on to others.

Because reliance on others and on several aspects of our environment is 'such a routine part of life, we very often trust without talking about it. Most of the time, it just happens' (Simpson 2012: 560). Indeed, as Simpson remarks, 'the actuality of trust may be very present, but it does not need to be talked unless there is some problem, and so trust is invisible' (Simpson 2012: 560). It is only when trust is broken, or we are facing the unfamiliar that trust surfaces in the conversation.

3.3 Wittgenstein on Distrust

Being such a basic stance, trust is the default for us. *Distrust*, for us, is like illness with respect to health: it is *not* our 'normal' condition. Wittgenstein makes this point time and again in OC. Here are some pertinent passages, in addition to the ones in OC (159–162) we have already encountered (Section 3.2); namely OC (219–223):

> There cannot be any doubt about it for me as a **reasonable** person.
> The **reasonable** man does *not* have certain doubts.
> Can I be in doubt **at will**?
> I cannot possibly doubt that I was never in the stratosphere.
> For mightn't I be crazy and not doubting what I absolutely ought to doubt?

What these and other passages make clear is that for Wittgenstein distrust and doubt are possible only when there are reasons and reasons are possible only if hinges stay put. Thus, trust is both a condition of possibility for, and prior to doubt and distrust. Starting with distrust or lack of trust would not be the most rational of moves. On the contrary, it would impede rationality and would border on insanity. To stress, we don't need reasons to trust hinges. Rather, the fact that we do trust hinges allows us to acquire reasons for or against ordinary empirical beliefs and therefore allows us to engage in those practices that are constitutive of epistemic rationality.

Therefore, it is only when the initial conditions for trust have been systematically or egregiously infringed upon that distrust is acceptable or justified (cf. also Lagerspetz 1998: 132–133). There is no quick and ready way of specifying when trust has been violated in this way, and therefore there is no easy way to establish when moving on to distrust *is* rational. As a rule of thumb, it may depend on our trust either being betrayed on multiple occasions and/or on significant issues, or indeed in conditions where we would routinely rely on people, objects, our faculties, and so on. Interestingly, from an epistemic point of view, if my sight and memory, which I usually trust, repeatedly let me down in what are generally considered normal conditions – when the lighting conditions are good, or when I am not intoxicated or affected by the posthumous effects of anaesthesia – then that rationally entitles me to distrust them. Whereas, if they let me down in abnormal conditions – when the room is too dark to see, or I am recovering from a concussion, say – then it would not be rational to move on to distrusting these faculties in general. Their occasional failure is entirely compatible with the fact that they remain trustworthy sources of information or of its retention, in the general run of cases.

Again, if in what seem to be normal conditions a person or even an expert gives me wrong information about topics in their purview, this makes it reasonable for me to stop trusting them, or even moving on to distrusting them (as sources of information at least in the area of discourse under consideration). By contrast, if the topic is not one they can be presumed to know or even be experts about, or conditions are not normal (e.g. they are intoxicated, under the effect of drugs, have just been injured, etc.) their passing on wrong information, at least on occasion, even on matters on which they may be presumed to be knowledgeable, is not sufficient to make it rational for me to stop trusting them or for me to start distrusting them, in general and/or with respect to their area of expertise.

Importantly, it is entirely consistent with what Wittgenstein says that hinges might also become the object of doubt and be abandoned over time, or in different contexts. Consider: it's normally a hinge for most of us that we have hands. We trust that much in all our acting and thinking. After a car accident, however, that might be overturned and we may have to distrust the deliverances of proprioception that may still make us feel as if we had our hands, like in the case of phantom limb syndrome.

Be that as it may, since trust is the default for us, it has 'ontological priority' over distrust (see Stern 2017) and it is 'axiologically' superior to distrust (Stern 2017). For it is the stance that allows us to operate best from an epistemic point of view (and beyond). This explains why, as a stance, trust can be maintained in the face of counterevidence, at least to some degree. That is, we are not justified to move on to distrust if our faculties, other people, institutions, or our environmental conditions have betrayed us once or only on occasion, or if the trust has been broken on non-fundamental issues, or in non-standard conditions.

Trust, however, can be broken, and, when this happens, the consequences can be disastrous. For turning to distrust can deeply affect the way people go through life and their being in the world (CV, 54). In fact, as stances towards life – that is, as ways of being in the world – trust and distrust may be appealed to in order to mark the difference between the world of the 'happy' and the world of the 'unhappy' (Wittgenstein 1921: 6.43). Whereas the world of the happy is one of openness and confidence with respect to others, the environment and even oneself, the world of the unhappy is one of closure, insularity, and diffidence regarding others or even one's own faculties. Distrust is therefore deeply dehumanizing.

3.4 The Bearing of Wittgenstein's Views on Current Debates about Trust

Current debates about trust focus on the attitude, rather than the content of it. Thus, it is only to be expected that no attention be paid to hinges *qua* what we acquire by trusting people, objects, institutions, and faculties, in the process of acquiring a language and our methods of inquiry.[33]

However, as we saw, what we may call 'hinge trust' refers to a specific stance that characterizes trust in its most basic, or *Ur-* form. It is this feature of Wittgenstein's account that has an important role to play in current debates about trust. For by looking at these debates, it is quite easy to get the impression of a problematic heterogeneity (Simpson 2012). Theorists seem to be interested in different things and somewhat artificially distinguish trust from reliance (see Goldberg 2020 for a discussion; the distinction was first introduced in Baier 1986), while such a distinction is hard to find in ordinary discourse or even practices and doesn't track across languages.

C. Thi Nguyen (2022) is a noticeable exception, and indeed his account of trust as an unquestioning attitude is very similar to Wittgenstein's. Nguyen, however, purports to distinguish between relying on and trusting objects and faculties. The key idea is that one may still rely on objects or faculties even if one doesn't trust them because one has no other or better option than to rely on them, at least on a specific occasion. Yet, from a Wittgensteinian perspective the real contrast would be between trusting or relying on objects or faculties, on the one hand, and simply making use of them because one has no other (or no

[33] Except for Lars Hertzberg (1988) and Olli Lagerspetz (1998), Wittgenstein scholars tend to be mostly interested in his account of the content of such trust, that is, hinges. See Wright (2004), Moyal-Sharrock (2005). Pritchard (2023) criticizes Wright (2004) for his account of trust in relation to hinges, when Wright's account of trust in OC is in fact at odds with Wittgenstein's. One stark difference between the two is that for Wright (and Pritchard who follows him), contrary to Wittgenstein, trust involves taking a risk and is rational only if warranted (either evidentially or non-evidentially). Pritchard agrees with that and therefore concludes that we shouldn't characterize our relationship to hinges as trust, but as an a-rational, visceral commitment. No need for such a revision would be motivated on Wittgenstein's actual account of trust, though.

better) option, on the other. When, in the absence of other or better options, we are forced to take our car to go somewhere, even when we know it isn't working properly, we are neither trusting nor relying on it to work properly. Rather, we are knowingly running the risk that it may not work as this is our only (or at least our best) option, given the circumstances.

Furthermore, contemporary theories of trust tend to focus narrowly on personal trust rather than on the general form of trust which, though it includes personal trust, also structures our relations to objects and faculties. While this can be motivated by the fact that many theorists working on trust have been interested in its moral implications, the fact remains that trust is not – at least not naturally – an attitude we have *only* towards people.

To characterize personal trust, then, contemporary theorists appeal to reactive attitudes, such as resentment and betrayal (Baier 1986, Holton 1994, Jones 1996), as conditions that would allow one to distinguish between mere reliance and (what by their lights is) trust, or even 'trust proper'.[34] Yet, reactive attitudes don't seem to be either necessary or sufficient for trust. For instance, one can trust someone to do something without resenting them (or feeling betrayed) for not complying with one's expectations, if the matter at hand is not particularly significant. Or else, one can resent them for not meeting one's expectations even if such expectations were not formed based on a relation of trust.

Of course, what we can elicit from *On Certainty* regarding hinge trust may be considered to be another kind of trust, which should be acknowledged alongside other forms of trust – especially 'personal' trust. Alternatively, the notion of hinge trust as a stance of openness and reliance on something/someone else may be taken to be fundamental also in the context of personal trust, and then used to specify more detailed conditions, which may or may not obtain in particular cases. For instance, I may be trusting you because you promised to φ; or because you undertook a commitment (which may have been incurred voluntarily, or because of occupying a certain social role, see Hawley (2019)); or because you are well-disposed towards me; and so on. These further specifications may then be taken to be constitutive of normatively *richer notions of trust* (Simpson 2012), such as 'personal' trust. Alternatively, as I prefer (Coliva 2025b), they may be considered constitutive of normatively *richer notions other than trust*, such as being a word-keeper, a good spouse or a friend, a collegial colleague, and so on.

Be that as it may, it is clear that if hinge trust is a stance, which does not constitutively involve doxastic propositional attitudes, like the (k-apt) belief that something or someone will do what we trust them to do, there will be at

[34] Sometimes, 'trust proper' is called 'personal/affective trust' and is contrasted with trust that is not 'trust proper', which is called 'predictive trust'. The latter, in turn, consists in predicting that someone will do thus-and-so.

least one notion of trust that is independent of such beliefs. This is important because it allows us to characterize infants 'thoroughgoing dependence on their parents as a paradigm kind of trust' (Simpson 2012: 559). Moreover, belief is rational only if backed up by reasons, but trust, at least hinge trust, is prior to the very possibility of offering reasons.

This, however, is also compatible with sometimes forming propositional attitudes of acceptance regarding what one trusts. For instance, if I trust that the floor will not disappear into the abyss, if I have the concepts necessary to consider the issue and I do consider the issue, I may assent to the corresponding proposition and even offer evidence in its support. Such evidence, however, is not the ground of my original trust. Thus, (*contra* Pritchard 2023) there is no bar to considering trust in hinges as an attitude of acceptance of them.

Finally, although the quantity of literature on distrust in relation to trust is modest, in it the point is often made that trust and distrust are contraries, not contradictories. That is, they are not exhaustive, for one may not trust someone without thereby distrusting them. Yet, they are mutually exclusive: if one trusts someone, then that is incompatible with distrusting them (at least in a given area) and vice versa.[35] Given that hinge trust is ontologically and axiologically superior to distrust, a Wittgensteinian approach to trust runs contrary to those theories, like Hawley's, that aim to shed light on trust by elucidating distrust.[36]

3.5 Conclusions

To conclude, paraphrasing Wittgenstein (OC 253), we may say that at the foundation of all well-founded beliefs (including testimonial ones) lies unfounded trust – that is, a non-epistemic and even non-propositional stance of openness and reliance towards our human and non-human environment. If, as Moyal-Sharrock (2005) argues, Wittgenstein's *On Certainty* is responsible for bringing the animal back into epistemology, it is with the basic stance of openness and reliance that characterizes hinge trust that the animal is brought back into epistemology in general and into the epistemology of testimony in particular.

Finally, since all hinges, insofar as they are constitutive of epistemic rationality, are acquired by trusting others and the world, the innovative aspect of Wittgenstein's proposal is that it isn't ratiocination that enables us to participate in epistemic practices wherein epistemic rationality unfolds but rather occupying such an unreflective stance. Thus, Wittgenstein's revolutionary move is not

[35] See Hawley (2019) and D'Cruz (2020).

[36] The important theme of when distrust is merited or not, especially when driven by identity prejudice against someone or a group, is discussed, in a broadly Wittgensteinian framework, by Anna Boncompagni (2021), Anna Pederneschi (2024), and Coliva (2025).

so much to have focused on the importance and primacy of action – Hume had already noticed that, outside the philosophy seminar, we act with a certainty that knows no doubt even if it cannot be supported by reasons. Rather, it is to have brought to light the fact that our animal, unreflective stance of openness and reliance onto others, our faculties, and the world is what allows us to acquire the hinges that are constitutive of epistemic rationality. That is, rationality and reasons would not – logically, and not just causally and genealogically – be possible without the animal; at least not for finite and social beings like us.[37]

4 Deep Disagreements and the Genealogical Challenge

> May someone have telling grounds for believing that the earth has only existed for a short time, say since his own birth? – Suppose he had always been told that, – would he have any good reason to doubt it? . . . Why should not a king be brought up in the belief that the world began with him? And if Moore and this king were to meet . . ., could Moore really prove his belief to be the right one? I do not say that Moore could not convert the king to his view, but it would be a conversion of a special kind; the king would be brought to look at the world in a different way.
>
> (OC 92)

4.1 Genealogical Challenges

An issue that has become prominent in contemporary social epistemology is the nature and bearing of so-called 'genealogical challenges'. I am using the plural here because, though there is often overlap, there are in fact three distinct kinds of genealogical challenges. Yet, for expository purposes, it is useful to keep them apart. First, there is the kind of genealogical challenge encapsulated in the 'you just believe that because . . . ' (YJBTB) schema (White 2010), also called 'etiological challenge'. Accordingly, some of our deep-seated beliefs seem to be more the product of causal factors – such as social, historical, or even political contingencies – than the result of a purely rational deliberation. As John Stuart Mill put it in *On Liberty* (1859: 17), the person who uncritically accepts the opinion of 'the world',

> devolves upon his own world the responsibility of being in the right against the dissentient worlds of other people; and it never troubles him that mere accident has decided which of these numerous worlds is the object of his reliance, and that the same causes which made him a churchman in London would have made him a Buddhist or a Confucian in Peking.

In recent years, diverging philosophical views, such as holding or rejecting the analytic/synthetic distinction (Cohen 2000), or one's large-scale political

[37] Cf. also Lagerspetz (1998: 7, 93–96).

commitments (Cohen 2000), have been considered good candidates for this kind of genealogical challenge. The gist of this kind of challenge, then, is that it is merely a causal contingency if we end up embracing one or the other of these views, rather than different and incompatible ones.

Another kind of genealogical challenge is the one raised by Bernard Williams (2002), Edward Craig (1991), Miranda Fricker (2007, 2008), and Thomas W. Simpson (2012) regarding some key concepts such as TRUTH, KNOWLEDGE, TESTIMONIAL JUSTICE, TRUST, and so on. This challenge suggests that, rather than look for sets of necessary and jointly sufficient conditions, which should give us, at once, the definition of these concepts and the essence common to all and only their instances, we should ask what these concepts are *for* – whence the name of 'pragmatic genealogies'. In carrying out this task, then, we may reconstruct or even invent genealogies to expose the key, or *Ur*- function these concepts (might have) subserve(d).

Finally, there is a third kind of genealogical challenge – usually raised by so-called 'critical genealogies' – to be found, most famously, but by no means exclusively, in the writings of Nietzsche and Foucault, which aims at (i) a debunking effect with respect to the alleged objectivity of moral values, sexual categories, madness, or even knowledge, and so on. By unravelling the (presumed) socio-political power structures from which moral or religious doctrines originated, or how sexuality, madness and even knowledge are socially constructed and certified, these genealogies also aim to show (ii) how these notions and doctrines subserve the purpose of perpetuating the dominance of those very power structures.

Wittgenstein's later writings are not concerned – at least not obviously – with this second aim of critical genealogies; whereas they relate to its first aim, which, arguably, overlaps with one of the goals of etiological challenges, at least in part. They are also connected with pragmatic genealogies. For, notoriously, Wittgenstein rejects definitional accounts of key concepts in philosophy and proposes instead a family-resemblance account of them (PI 65–77).[38] He equally rejects the idea that there is an essence common to all and only the items that fall under such concepts. Furthermore, his methodological use of imagination to either show some key, allegedly original, and possibly simpler function some concepts may have played (PI 2–8), or how our concepts could have been different, in dissimilar natural and social scenarios, represents an important ancestor of this second kind of genealogy.

[38] The notion of family resemblance, in its turn, is inspired by Goethe's morphological method, developed in the *Metamorphosis of Plants* (1870), with the attendant idea of an *Ur-Pflanz* from which all vegetal forms would derive. For a discussion of the relationship between Wittgenstein and Goethe, via the mediation of Friedrich Waismann, see Coliva (2024g).

In the following, we will examine Wittgenstein's reflections in *On Certainty* and their relationship to the etiological form of genealogical critique, paying particular attention to its debunking aim, which, as we have noted, is also a goal of critical genealogies. The connection is quite obvious, for, as we saw (Section 2), hinges are inherited from our community (like religious or political views); they are 'hammered' into us through education in formal and informal settings (like religion or large-scale political or philosophical views); they may change or evolve through time and space and are therefore variable (like religious, political, or philosophical views); and they constitute our image of the world, but such an image may be different for others – diachronically or even synchronically – like in the aforementioned areas of human inquiry and experience. Moreover, constituting an image of the world, and being the conditions of possibility of producing reasons for or against ordinary empirical beliefs, they may not change through argumentation – reasons come to an end and crucially presuppose the very hinges one party is upholding and the other one is rejecting, thus being rationally inert for the latter. A change of hinges, therefore, may only take the form of a conversion (like in the religious case, and possibly in the political or even in the philosophical one). Thanks to such a conversion, we are brought to look at the world differently (like in the religious case, and possibly also in politics and philosophy).

This kind of genealogical challenge is, therefore, a leitmotif of *On Certainty*, and seems to open the door to epistemic relativism, at least prima facie. For, insofar as reasons depend on hinges and hinges are variable and mutually incompatible, upholding a certain picture of the world is a matter of contingency, due to social or historical factors. Had we been born and raised differently, we would likely have had a different picture of the world and would thus recognize as rational (or irrational) other, incompatible sets of ordinary empirical beliefs, which would depend on holding on to other, incompatible hinges. Indeed, the whole of rationality – determined by our practices of asking/giving reasons – seems to rest on causally determined, and potentially variable – that is, contingent – hinges.

4.2 Deep Disagreement and Kinds of Relativism

In recent years, much attention has been devoted to the problem of disagreement among epistemic peers. Epistemic peers share epistemic methods and are assumed to be equally rational and knowledgeable with respect to the topic at issue. Classic examples involve returning opposite verdicts about how much is owed, when splitting a bill. The question then is raised when, once's faced with a peer disagreement, one should be steadfast in one's belief or else lower one's credence.

As we saw in Section 4.1, many passages in *On Certainty* raise a different but related issue; namely, how to react to a disagreement about hinges – and in particular, whether a rational response is at all possible, when faced with such a disagreement. For, first, if hinges constitute epistemic methods, hinge disagreements raise the issue of when we could consider subjects or groups as epistemic peers, because, by holding on to different hinges, parties to this kind of disagreement would not share epistemic methods and couldn't be considered to be epistemic peers.

Secondly, as observed by Robert Fogelin (1985: 6): 'the possibility of a genuine argumentative exchange depends [. . .] on the fact that together we accept many things.' Consequently, disagreements over hinges 'cannot be resolved through the use of argument, for they undercut the conditions essential to arguing.'

Finally, there are issues that stem from the distinctive metaphysical-cum-epistemological profile of hinge propositions. For, as we saw in Section 2, Wittgenstein regarded hinges as neither true nor false (OC 196–206, at least in robustly truth-theoretical terms); as neither justified nor unjustified (OC 110, 130, 166; or at least as neither in need of further justification nor as held against justification); as neither known nor unknown (OC 121, at least in an epistemic or empirical sense of 'to know'); and as neither rational nor irrational (OC 559, at least if rationality depends on being supported by justifications and evidence). Since disagreement involves taking opposite stances with respect to the truth, or the justification, or the knowability of a given content, it then becomes dubious that when there is a hinge clash there is also a genuine case of *disagreement*. Rather, there seems to be more of a case of *deep distance* between parties to the conflict.[39]

This issue, then, clearly bears on whether *On Certainty* ends up proposing a form of epistemic relativism, and, in turn, whether Wittgenstein was inclined towards a relativism characterized by faultless *disagreement*, or towards a relativism of *distance*.[40] The question is whether hinge-disagreements involve two parties reaching incompatible and ultimately contradictory conclusions about the same propositional content, with neither being at fault from a third-person perspective, as in a disagreement over whether sushi is tasty. Alternatively, we might question whether such disagreements arise because each party's position is inaccessible or unavailable to the other, so that what counts as reasonable for one party is not reasonable for the other, due to their differing perspectives. This would be similar to certain ethical judgments, where opposing views depend on

[39] Coliva and Palmira (2020) develops an account of hinges that allows for them to be minimally truth-apt. Some of Wittgenstein's own remarks in *On Certainty* point in that direction too. That would allow for at least the possibility of a genuine disagreement over hinges.

[40] See Baghramian and Coliva (2020) for details regarding these two different forms of relativism and their relations.

being situated within different, de facto inaccessible moral frameworks, like the contrast between medieval samurai ethics and contemporary Western ethics, as famously discussed by Bernard Williams.

By paying close attention to the differences among hinges, as well as to Wittgenstein's account of hinge-truth and hinge-rationality, a nuanced response may be returned to these interrelated issues. In fact, it may be argued that while there is a positional difference between those who hold that nobody has ever been on the Moon – like Wittgenstein – and those who don't – like us – this is not by itself a reason to think that, according to Wittgenstein's view in *On Certainty*, there wouldn't be a way of rationally resolving the disagreement (see OC 106–108). For we are sharing the same 'system' – roughly, the one constituted by science – within which progress is possible.

Yet, for other hinges and possible disagreement about them, where altogether different systems of evidence are concerned, Wittgenstein's views are more hospitable to relativism, in the form of a relativism of distance. Connectedly, that shows that within his framework, genealogical challenges are epistemologically salient only when disagreements of this latter kind are at stake (OC 608–612). In these cases, no rational resolution is possible, and persuasion (OC 262, 612) and conversion (OC 92) will have to take place, to allow one party to the debate to move over to the other party's system of hinges.

4.3 Varieties of Hinges and of Reasons for Fitting into the YJBTB Schema

Here is a Table 1 with some notable hinges and some considerations for having them fit into the YJBTB – 'You just believe that because . . . ' – schema.

Table 1 Varieties of hinges

'No one has ever been on the Moon' (OC 106, 108, 171, 286)	YJBTB you lived before 1969	Had you lived after 1969 you would not have believed it.
'The Earth is flat' (OC 85)	YJBTB you lived long before the scientific revolution; or are part of a (conspiracy) group that has no trust in science	Had you lived after wards you would have not believed it. You would not believe it if you were not part of a conspiracy group.

Table 1 (cont.)

'The Earth has been created (by God) in less than 7 days' (OC 336)	YJBTB you have been raised in a creationist community	Had you not been raised in a creationist community you would not believe it.
'God exists' (OC 107)	YJBTB you have been raised in a theistic community	Had you not been raised in a theistic community you would not believe it
'There are physical objects' (OC 35–37, 53–55, 57–59, 447, 454) 'There is an external world' (OC 20, 338)	YJBTB you have been raised in a community that speaks the 'thing-language'.	Had you not been raised in a community that speaks the 'thing-language' you would not believe it.

4.3.1 Harmless Instances of 'YJBTB It's a Hinge'

While all hinges present on this table fit into the YJBTB schema, they are importantly different. As noted by Yuval Avnur and Dion Scott-Kakures (2015) and G. A. Cohen (2000), at least 'No one has ever been on the Moon', and possibly other hinges like it, such as 'The Sun revolves around the Earth', and 'The Earth was created in less than 7 days', may be believed because of one's position in history. For instance, before the development of the technology necessary to fly to the Moon, it was perfectly fine to hold on to such a hinge, or even to 'No one will ever go to the Moon'. Simply, around 1969, the possibility of flying to the Moon became salient and finally realized itself. What used to be a hinge, got demoted to the role of ordinary empirical proposition, and became susceptible to epistemic and semantic evaluation.

These instances of the YJBTB schema are not epistemically problematic. They only point to the fact that when and where one was born and raised may play a significant role with respect to one's access to knowledge and justification. Yet none of them calls into question the fact that *knowledge and justification are in fact possessed* when one is lucky enough to have been born and raised at certain times or in certain places. Moreover, if one were not born in such circumstances but were exposed to the relevant evidence, together with the kind of scientific methodology that supports it, one would have had access to such justification and knowledge too.

Hence, one of the required factors for an epistemically problematic instance of the YJBTB schema isn't just the awareness of there being a culture or group that believes an incompatible hinge (or proposition). Rather, the disagreement should become a defeater of one's justification, or, at the very least, reveal the problematic character of one's justification for the proposition believed.

At any rate, the existence of religious and conspiracy groups that still hold on to some of those once-upon-a-time hinges is in no way a reason *for us* to doubt that we do know better. That is, awareness of such an alternative culture or group does not defeat *our* justification to believe that someone has been on the Moon; nor does the existence of said group call into question the legitimacy of our justification for having formed this belief in the first place.

Interestingly, Wittgenstein maintains the very same conclusion (albeit relative to what was a hinge at his time, that is, 'No one has ever been on the Moon'). As he writes in OC 286 (cf. 264):

> What we believe depends on what we learn. We all believe that it isn't possible to get to the moon; but there might be people who believe that that is possible and that it sometimes happens. We say: these people do not know a lot that we know. And, let them be never so sure of their belief – they are wrong and we know it. If we compare our system of knowledge with theirs then theirs is evidently the poorer one by far.

Yet, as we saw, our system of knowledge can (at least in principle) be shared with those who don't possess it. Thus, becoming aware of it, for those who were not born and raised within it, would (or should) prompt an assessment of their own reasons for holding otherwise and would (or should) lead to rational change.

Furthermore, this kind of disagreement should not lead to any form of epistemic relativism, for Wittgenstein. Within science, we may occupy different stages of its development, and this does not give rise to any 'faultless disagreement' or – even less – incommensurability: had those reasons been available before, they would have been rationally relevant and parties to the debate would have agreed. As Wittgenstein himself points out (OC 108), believing that one could go to the Moon would require 'answers to the questions "How did he overcome the force of gravity?" "How could he live without an atmosphere?" and a thousand others which could not be answered' at Wittgenstein's time, but that found an answer soon afterwards. Furthermore, these reasons are essentially developed within the same epistemic system, so they are not (wouldn't have been) incommensurable, or invisible, irrelevant, or inaccessible, to the other party to the debate.

4.3.2 Problematic Instances of YJBTB It's a Hinge

Let's consider other hinges Wittgenstein discusses, such as 'God exists'. Consider what in OC 336 Wittgenstein writes – mistakenly, in my view – about creationism, which, when *On Certainty* was written, was already a *passé* doctrine:

> But what men consider reasonable or unreasonable alters. At certain periods men find reasonable what at other periods they found unreasonable. And vice-versa. But is there no objective character here? *Very* intelligent and well-educated people believe in the story of creation in the Bible, while others hold it as proven false, and the grounds of the latter are well known to the former.

Now, independently of the application to creationism, this passage contains a deep intuition, regarding the problematic raised by fitting into the YJBTB schema, from an epistemic point of view.

First, what is relevant is the existence of a disagreement between parties concerning a putative hinge. Here it is important to keep in mind the distinction between disagreement as a state and disagreement as an activity (McFarlane 2014). While we may disagree with someone in the disagreement-as-an-activity-sense only if we have a real debate with them, we may disagree with someone in the disagreement-as-a-state sense and also with someone we never met or could never meet. Thus, I could disagree with Wittgenstein in the latter sense because I hold views incompatible with his; and I could disagree with the members of a hypothetical community that for instance believes that water's chemical structure is XYZ, instead of H_2O, even if this community exists only counterfactually.

Second, what is required is knowledge of the fact the other party has reasons – better, evidence, in the case of hinges – for holding on to such a hinge or for discarding it. Third, and contrary to 'Nobody has ever been on the Moon', such reasons – or evidence – are not enough to *conclusively* establish the hinge, or for discarding it. This isn't due to the paucity of evidence, which could be remedied in the future, as in the case of the hinges we considered in the previous section. Rather, it is due to the fact that the reasons for a given hinge are either circular, or question-begging against, or no stronger than the reasons for discarding it, or even irrelevant within a different worldview.

Now, plug in 'God exists' *in lieu* of the creationist hinge. This fourth element of the epistemic problematic raised by fitting into the YJBTB schema becomes evident, especially in the light of Wittgenstein's own treatment of religion.[41] For

[41] Since the *Tractatus Logico-Philosophicus*, up to *On Certainty*, via the *Lectures on Religious Belief*, and many entries in *Culture and Value*, Wittgenstein has been concerned with the nature of religious belief and the status of 'God exists', which, much like 'There are physical objects' (see Section 4.5), he considers playing a grammatical role, rather than a descriptive one. Against this background, the believer and the non-believer, who take that statement to be a description, which the believer affirms, and the non-believer denies, are bound to appeal to evidence that will

him, there are no non-circular or *non-question-begging reasons* – or evidence – that can be adduced to decide the issue of God's existence. (Or at the very least one's reasons are no stronger than one's opponent's). Thus, for the significance of the genealogical challenge, it matters *why* we disagree (Mogensen 2016). To stress, the reason for the disagreement must reside in the nature of the topic under dispute: it must be the case that the topic does not allow for rational resolution via *principled reasons.*

To illustrate: if the religious believer appeals to the Bible as evidence in favour of God's existence, then the non-believer will be quick to point out that the Bible may exert that epistemic authority only if it is the revealed word of God, which presupposes trusting in God's existence already. Thus, the appeal to the Bible to prove the existence of God is question-begging against the non-believer. Yet, the believer would insist that the Bible is not just like any other piece of historical evidence, the reliability of which may be questioned. Rather, it is the word of God and should thus be taken at face value as manifesting God's existence, word, and will. Hence, denying or being agnostic about that is question-begging against the believer.

Furthermore, a believer and a non-believer could agree on their account of Nature and its efficient causes (as it may happen between two physicists, for instance) and yet the former may appeal to a different kind of evidence – what, following Blaise Pascal, in his *Pensées*, we may call 'the evidence of the heart' (1958: 277, 282), which is an ensemble of experiences and feelings – to support their faith, as a direct manifestation of God and his benevolence. A non-believer need not deny the kinds of experience salient to the believer, but would likely consider them as merely psychological, rather than revelatory in kind. For those experiences to count as manifestations of God, God's existence will have to be assumed, and this is clearly question-begging against the non-believer. The believer, however, will insist that they are tangible manifestations of God's existence and so the non-believer's denial will be question-begging against the believer.

Finally, a believer may appeal to God as what guarantees the possibility of providing an answer to fundamental questions about *final causes*, such as 'Why is there something rather than nothing?', 'Why do I exist?', 'Why do living creatures have to suffer?', and so on. And here the non-believer will simply be indifferent to such questions: either these why-questions are interpreted as questions about the *efficient causes* of the universe, our own existence, or the existence of pain; or else they have no right of citizenship in their worldview and would be question-begging insofar as they would be interpreted as calling for

be considered question-begging by the other party. For a comprehensive introduction to Wittgenstein's philosophy of religion, see Schönbaumsfeld (2023). For a development of a religious hinge epistemology, see Coliva, Pritchard, and Schönbaumsfeld (ms).

transcendental final causes. Yet, the believer will insist that there is no reason to confine oneself only to efficient and non-transcendental final causes. Thus, the non-believer's position is question-begging with respect to the believer.

In short, in this case the absence of reasons or evidence that could be used to (epistemically) rationally resolve the disagreement is not a contingent fact, due to one's positioning in history, or in the 'knowledge economy', where reasons and evidence are often possessed only by specific individuals, groups or even cultures, often insulated from one another, yet shareable in principle at least. Rather, the absence of such reasons or evidence is a necessary feature of the disagreement, since those reasons would be question-begging against one's opponents, or no stronger than theirs and not further improvable, or indeed would have no place within the other party's worldview. Thus, calling the ensemble of hinges – properly so-regarded – a '*picture*' of the world (OC 93–94) is apposite: we are not and cannot be rationally convinced to go over to different hinges. Either we *see* things a certain way or we don't. Only a kind of *conversion* could bring us to *see* things differently.

It is only when the propositions fitting into the YJBTB schema fulfil these conditions, that the realization that we just believe them because we were so brought up undermines the epistemic credentials we thought we had for holding on to them. In fact, it shows that for all our evidence, those propositions could not be proved by means of it, for that evidence is epistemically powerless if those propositions are not already assumed. Or said otherwise, it is only when we witness a *deep* disagreement with someone that fitting into the YJBTB schema signals an epistemic problem. To repeat, deep disagreement is a disagreement with someone who does not hold our hinges, while there is no stronger or non-question-begging evidence that could be used to convince them otherwise.

Saying that being a problematic instance of the YJBTB schema signals the presence of deep disagreement means acknowledging the derivative nature of the genealogical challenge. That is, genealogical challenges are no different in kind from cases of deep disagreement. In turn, as we have seen, deep disagreements aren't merely disagreements just about important issues or simply about hinges. On the contrary, they are disagreements about hinges wherein the disagreement lacks a solution in principle given the kinds of evidence to which the parties would appeal; namely, evidence which would be either circular, question-begging, or no-stronger than the evidence at the other party's disposal.

Yet, fitting into this schema brings out the characteristic causal story that is responsible for our having the hinges we do in fact have, which typically remains in the background when epistemologists deal with deep disagreement as such. That is, it brings out the fact that our hinges and worldview are inherited from a community, which is kept together by such a shared worldview. This, in turn, may explain why, in the absence of decisive epistemic reasons for or against it, we are within our rights in holding on to it. That is, our loyalty to the community may be a decisive *pragmatic* reason for us to maintain it.

Furthermore, as we have seen, in these cases, there seems to be an incommensurability between what counts as evidence for what. Consider the proposition 'God exists': one party takes the testimony of the Bible, the evidence of the heart, or questions about final causes as relevant to holding that hinge in place. The other party treats 'God exists' as an empirical proposition and holds that the kind of evidence appealed to by the believer would have a bearing on the determination of its truth, only if we took for granted that God exists and that the Bible is his revealed word, or that those characteristic experiences manifest God's existence and love, or that there can be transcendental final causes. The existence of these problematic instances of the YJBTB schema thus reveals a connection between the genealogical challenge and relativism, in the form of a *relativism of distance*. That is, there is a 'gulf', or unbridgeable gap between these different worldviews. It also shows that what is crucial to the latter isn't the adoption of a different conceptual scheme (*à la* Davidson), which typically drives the idea of incommensurability often associated with conceptual relativism. After all, the parties perfectly understand each other. Rather, they hold on to different and incompatible hinges and to different and incompatible systems of evidence and proof, which then license as justified or (unjustified) different and incompatible beliefs.

If this is right, then we may profitably take Wittgenstein's views to bear on the contemporary debate on the nature of the genealogical challenge. Clearly, they align with those accounts that consider the genealogical challenge derivative with respect to the issue of disagreement, such as White (2010). Still, this per se is not sufficient to give rise to a distinctive epistemic problem. For, if you and I disagree about how much we owe when we split the bill, there is a perfectly agreed-upon procedure to decide the issue, such that at most one of us is right (assuming we had previously agreed to share the bill evenly). Moreover, if you and Wittgenstein disagreed about whether anyone has ever been on the Moon, you would still have telling grounds and decisive evidence to prove that you are right, and he is wrong. So, even if Wittgenstein happened to believe that no one did because he died almost twenty years before the Moon landing, this is no reason to call into question the epistemic credentials of *your* belief. Furthermore, those epistemic credentials would have presumably led him to believe the same, had he been aware of them.

Rather, by following Wittgenstein's discussion, we realize that it is only when the disagreement runs deeper – that is, there are no non-circular, non-question-begging or stronger reasons to hold on to a hinge proposition – that fitting into the

YJBTB schema signals an important epistemic problem. For, if there are no such non-question-begging epistemic reasons, then if there are reasons at all, they are produced within a system of assumptions, or hinges, that the other party has no epistemic reason to accept, even if they were made aware of them.

4.4 The Rationality of YJBTB There Are Physical Objects Because It's a Hinge

Based on our discussion so far, one might be led to think that, for Wittgenstein, the application of the YJBTB schema to 'There is an external world' or 'There are physical objects' is also epistemically problematic. Yet, here is what Wittgenstein has to say about 'There are physical objects' in OC (35–37):

> But can't it be imagined that there should be no physical objects? I don't know. And yet "There are physical objects" is nonsense. Is it supposed to be an empirical proposition? – And is *this* an empirical proposition: "There seem to be physical objects"?
>
> "A is a physical object" is a piece of instruction which we give only to someone who doesn't yet understand either what "A" means, or what "physical object" means. Thus it is instruction about the use of words, and "physical object" is a **logical concept**. (Like colour, quantity . . .) And that is why no such proposition as: "There are physical objects" can be formulated. Yet we encounter such unsuccessful shots at every turn.
>
> But is it adequate to answer to the scepticism of the idealist, or the assurances of the realist, to say that "There are physical objects" is nonsense? For them after all it is not nonsense. It would, however, be an answer to say: this assertion, or its opposite is a misfiring attempt to express what can't be expressed like that. And that it does misfire can be shown; but that isn't the end of the matter. We need to realize that what presents itself to us as the first expression of a difficulty, or of its solution, may as yet not be correctly expressed at all.

Thus, 'There are physical objects' should not be interpreted as a description – as a statement about what there is. Interpreted that way, as the realist and the idealist do, it is nonsense, for Wittgenstein. However, it is not nonsense if interpreted as a grammatical statement about the fact that, in our language, we countenance such a 'logical' (OC 36) concept (as well as other 'logical', or 'formal', or 'categorial' concepts, such as COLOR, QUANTITY, etc.).[42] Thanks to such a 'logical concept' certain inferences concerning the continued existence of instances of that category (in fact, instances of *sortal* concepts falling under

[42] What Wittgenstein here calls a 'logical concept' is strongly connected to what he considered to be 'formal concepts' in the *Tractatus*. For a discussion of the development of his views on this topic, see Coliva (2024b).

that formal concept, such as tables and chairs, etc.) even when they are not perceived are licensed, whereas other kinds of inference are forbidden.

Taken as a descriptive statement, the reasons appealed to by the realist are question-begging against the idealist and vice versa. Even their respective starting points, such as, on the one hand, the certainty of there being a hand here – *à la* Moore – or merely an experience as of a hand – *à la* the idealist (or phenomenalist) – would be question-begging against the opponent. Hence, taken as a descriptive statement, 'There are physical objects' would fit into the YJBTB schema and would produce a problematic instantiation of it.

When understood as a grammatical statement about the type of language we in fact use and the kinds of inferences the statement 'There are physical objects' permits or prohibits, it becomes clear that this is what enables us to transcend our cognitive locality. For it allows us to use our current experiences or memories to justify beliefs about specific objects, even when we are not perceiving them directly, have never perceived them, or will no longer be able to do so in the future.

Now, the important point is that the very possibility of having justifications and reasons for and against ordinary empirical statements understood as being about mind-independent objects depends on taking for granted the hinge 'There are physical objects'. Thus, while it is true, for Wittgenstein, that we just believe that there are physical objects because we have been brought up in a community that speaks a language that countenances that logical concept, taking that hinge for granted is a condition of possibility for producing reasons and justifications for ordinary empirical statements, and is therefore constitutive of epistemic rationality. That is why holding on to it is rationally legitimate, even in the absence of non-circular evidence in favour of it.

4.5 Conclusions

While Wittgenstein's hinges fit into the YJBTB schema because they have been inculcated in us through enculturation, and despite their possible cultural and historical variability, they do not always give rise to epistemically problematic instances of that schema. When hinges such as 'No one has ever been on the Moon' or 'The Earth is flat' are plugged into that schema, they merely show a positional difference that doesn't undermine justification and knowledge when in fact possessed (in this case for the opposite views). When, in contrast, hinges like 'There are physical objects' are plugged in, given that they are conditions of possibility for epistemic rationality altogether, their fitting into the YJBTB schema is compatible with their being rationally held, despite not being supported by evidential reasons. However, when we plug into the YJBTB schema other culturally variable hinges, like 'God exists', which aren't constitutive of (epistemic) rationality, the awareness that reasons for them would be question-begging against an opponent or at least no stronger than theirs reveals that, while we may adduce evidence in their favour, that evidence is not going to settle the issue against one's opponent and for principled reasons. Of course, that does not make those hinges and precepts any less important to us and to our identity. Yet, it shows that some of our deepest convictions belong more to the way we *see* things than to the way things are, or indeed must be seen for epistemic rationality to be possible. Realizing that in different circumstances we would likely have had different ones shows, in its turn, that at least in these cases relativism – in the form of a relativism of distance – remains an option.

5 'I Am a Woman'

> That I am a man and not a woman can be verified, but if I were to say I was a woman, and then tried to explain the error by saying I hadn't checked the statement, the explanation would not be accepted. The *truth* of my statements is the test of my understanding of these statements.
>
> (OC 79–80)

Much attention has been devoted in recent years to the concept of WOMAN, both in connection with ameliorative projects in conceptual engineering (Haslanger 2012), and with respect to the role of self-identification in the determination of gender (Butler 1988), as well as regarding trans identities (Bettcher 2012). Concomitantly, a 'feminist wave' in Wittgenstein studies has taken place (Scheman and O'Connor 2002, Tanesini 2004, O'Connor 2008, Scheman 2011, Ashton 2019, Boncompagni 2024 a, b, Laugier, Provost, and Trächtler 2022, Coliva 2025a, d, Moyal-Sharrock and Sandis 2024). This section explores some of the possible interconnections between these trends by proposing a Wittgenstein-inspired treatment of some key issues.

As a preliminary, it should be noted that Wittgenstein's approach to language is notoriously descriptivist. It enjoins to look at how we use the relevant terms and is not directly engaged with their revision. That is, it does not hold that philosophers, *qua* philosophers, are better placed than other individuals in the society at large, to revise current concepts, either to pass them on to society, or to expose forms of subordination and/or discrimination present in the society against some of its members.[43] For this reason, as we saw in Section 1.3, it is often considered unserviceable in the context of social critique. Correctly understood, however, it is only inimical to the idea that this critique could be

[43] *Contra* ameliorative projects inspired by a more Carnapian conception of language and its philosophy (Carnap 1950), such as Haslanger (2012). See Coliva (2025a) for a discussion.

carried out by proposing linguistic and conceptual changes merely from the philosophical armchair, as it were. To be effective, these changes need to take place in the actual linguistic usage, as it develops out of societal needs and pressures. Of course, philosophers are part of society and can be engaged in these dynamics, but they do not occupy a specific vantage point by virtue of being philosophers (of language or mind), for him.

That said, there are several Wittgensteinian 'tools', to be found especially in the *Philosophical Investigations* and in *On Certainty*, that can be put at the service of making (better) sense of ongoing societal issues having to do with gender. One of the key tools to be found in the later Wittgenstein is the notion of family resemblance, which, as we shall see (Section 5.1), can be put to service to make better sense of women and trans women's lived experiences than approaches that would define the concept WOMAN based on allegedly essential biological, or even social features that all and only women would share.

Secondly, Wittgenstein's view of first-personal psychological avowals as grammatically authoritative, as well as his view of 'I am a man/woman' as a (personal) hinge (OC 79–83), may be used to support the constitutive role of self-identification with respect to gender determination, even when one's gender may not be coincident with one's natal sex (Section 5.2).

Finally, his views regarding such a hinge may help us better understand present-day political conflict over these issues as a clash between two hinges 'Gender is/isn't coincident with natal sex' such that any discrepancy is/isn't to be considered a pathological deviation. Arguably, this may also help illuminate the political significance of the practice, to be found in several Western societies, of leaving it to subjects to determine their gender and, with it, the pronouns they want others to use to refer to them (Section 5.2).

5.1 WOMAN as a Family-Resemblance Concept

A Wittgensteinian approach to questions such as 'what is a woman?' or 'who counts as a woman?' is predicated on the idea that meanings are arbitrary, and that often issues that seem to take the form of metaphysical questions into the nature of reality are better approached by looking at the workings of the corresponding words or concepts. For meanings and concepts are not set in stone: they are the result of certain social conventions, and they may change over time. Hence, a Wittgensteinian approach is anti-essentialist, if by 'essence' we mean a *natural* essence (or even a *social* essence, or kind).

First, according to a Wittgensteinian approach, concepts or meanings aren't always determined by explicit definitions. Sometimes, clearly, they are – like in the mathematical, the scientific or in the legal context. Yet, when we are interested in the terms and concepts that people in our societies use in their everyday interactions, then that approach is often unavailable. The way in which people typically use these terms is rather through *family resemblance*.

Developing this idea, one might then propose that the meaning of 'woman' should be identified through family resemblance rather than through a set of necessary and jointly sufficient conditions. Accordingly, there would be people who are considered instances of the concept in question and then other ones would be taken to fall under the concept, if they share *one or the other* of the features of these cases, but not necessarily all or a (weighted) majority of them.[44]

There is considerable controversy about how best to understand family resemblance, even in the context of its possible application to WOMAN. Some theorists (Stoljar 1995: 282–286, 2011: 42, Hale 1996, Bettcher 2012: 237, 241), for instance, think that it would depend on sharing some focal features, with the attendant difficulty of (i) determining what they are; and (ii) allowing for cases of being 'more' or 'less' women, thus creating a problem for the proper inclusion of some people into this category, not least lesbians and trans women.

Yet, as Friedrich Waismann explained the notion of family resemblance, borrowing Wittgenstein's example of GAME: 'it may be merely that *every two games are connected by intermediate links*' (1965: 82). That is, like tennis is a game which cannot be played alone and where there is winning and losing, so is solitaire, where there is winning and losing but which can be played alone, and so is playing with dolls, which can be played alone and where there is no winning or losing. Solitaire is therefore the intermediate link that connects tennis and playing with dolls, even though these latter games may have nothing in common between them.

This explains the relevance of intermediate links for Wittgenstein (PI 122). Like the intermediate links in a chain connect separate links, which do not touch each other in any point, intermediate instances of a concept *C* serve to unite instances that may have nothing in common between them, and they do so by means of having (at least) one feature in common with each of these separate instances, though not the same one(s).

One might then think that if something is a game then it must be an enjoyable activity for those who engage in it. Surely, this is often the case, but it need not be. That is, there are games which people play even if they don't find them enjoyable, and there are many activities people enjoy doing that aren't games.

[44] Family resemblance, in fact, isn't a prototype theory (cf. Rosch & Mervis (1975)). However useful the latter might be to explain typicality effects, and no matter whether their proponents were inspired by the notion of family resemblance, they remain different ways of conceiving of meanings and concepts. I discuss the interplay between concepts, prototypes, and stereotypes in connection with WOMAN in Coliva (2024c, 2025a).

The difficulty here is to fully grasp the idea that, from a metaphysical point of view, there are no barriers to inclusion within a family-resemblance concept, at least in principle. Still, this does not mean that, in practice, 'anything goes'. For the process will be driven by our actual needs. Thus, it is unlikely that, say, we will want to include tables and chairs under the concept WOMAN, while it is more likely that, if AI keeps developing at the rate it does, and if our lives will be more and more intertwined with those of robots, we might have to consider the issue of their inclusion within such (and related categories) in a not-too-distant future.

This more inclusive account of family resemblance is important for several reasons. First, as anticipated, it avoids the idea that one should count as a woman only if certain traits are shared, and connectedly, that there would be individuals who would be more of a woman than others, if they shared more of these traits or more of the 'heavy-weight' ones. Thus, contrary to prototype theories of concepts, not having some 'heavy-weight' traits shared by focal members of a class, does not determine exclusion from it, even if it may explain why it may take us longer to subsume those instances under the relevant concepts.

Secondly, family resemblance clarifies in what sense concepts are *open-ended*. Since inclusion within a concept does not depend on sharing a specific set of predetermined features, but only resemblance in some respect, it is possible to include new elements, as long as they resemble already included ones. Thus, one important aspect of family resemblance is that it allows for the *extension* of the concept *to new cases*, in potentially *unpredictable* ways.

Thirdly, family resemblance should not be conflated with vagueness. That is, the proposed account of WOMAN does not depend on the fact that biologically there may be human beings that fall in between male and female, or have some biological features of both, such that the concept WOMAN would not be a clear-cut one.[45] The point, rather, is that if WOMAN works by family resemblance, the criteria for inclusion within the class of women – however subject to vagueness they might be – may expand over time to become more inclusive.

Finally, the concept WOMAN, on this proposal, *remains one*, while evolving through time. That is, no replacement of meaning/concept is affected simply by adding new criteria for membership within the concept. Rather, the concept WOMAN would be a potentially open-ended, revisable overlap of features that have entered the concept through time (PI 67–68). Our definitions, therefore, would only be snapshots of moments in the life of the concept – corresponding to (sometimes overlapping) temporal stages of one single concept. They may serve very useful purposes, like in the legal or scientific context, but context and

[45] See Stoljar (1995: 269) and Kapusta (2017) for a discussion of intermediate cases and their bearing on WOMAN.

purpose are inevitably historically determined. Thus, we should not mistake the concept in its entirety with any of its temporal stages. Furthermore, the open-endedness of the concept leaves room for its extension to new cases which are not presently considered simply because they may not be salient at this time in history. In fact, the criteria[46] for inclusion within the class determined by the concept may be expanded. In that sense, the very same concept would be changed, just like an individual, thought of as a spatio-temporal worm, can change its properties while remaining one and the same.

Importantly, these more inclusive criteria would not necessarily entail identity in function – be it 'natural' or 'social'. Thus, on a Wittgensteinian approach, we could still have the same concept WOMAN and yet ameliorate *it*, in the sense that, for instance, we would be expanding it to new cases such as trans women. We would be doing so while keeping the *same* concept: simply, new cases that were not initially considered to fall under that concept are now considered to be included under *it*.

A Wittgensteinian approach not only makes sense of the idea of ameliorating our existing concept, instead of simply replacing it,[47] but is also *politically* apt. For activists in favour of considering trans women women are fighting for including the former into that very concept. They are not asking us to consider them women in a different sense.[48] As Talia Mae Bettcher puts it (2012: 233): 'Being a trans woman is not a strange type of woman, but a woman, period'.[49] In this sense, a Wittgensteinian conception of WOMAN allows us to redress forms of hermeneutical injustice (Fricker 2007, but see also Coliva 2025c) which don't permit trans people to make sense to themselves and/or others of their lived experience, due to identity prejudice against them.

---

[46] Criteria are neither necessary nor sufficient conditions traditionally understood, but the 'hooks' by means of which concepts work, under the family resemblance model, and by means of which concepts can be extended to cover new and unprecedented cases.

[47] This is the worry often raised against Carnapian approaches, which by replacing the existing concept with another one, would be changing the subject and would not be ameliorating the actual concept.

[48] Other examples of political battles to be included within the same category are those in favour of same-sex marriage, where spouses want to be considered husband or wife in the same sense as husbands and wives in heterosexual marriages. See also Moyal-Sharrock and Sandis (2024) for other examples.

[49] Clearly, it will be for stakeholders to determine what suits their goals best. Here I am assuming that one goal voiced by at least some trans women is that of full inclusion within the class of women. There may be other goals, and there may even be disagreement among members of the same group with respect to what these goals are. Furthermore, it should not be inferred that a more inclusive concept WOMAN would pre-empt the need for non-cis categories or would necessarily be detrimental to the recognition of cis women's rights. No more than the existence of adopted children, say, would pre-empt the idea of biological ones or be detrimental to the rights of the latter.

According to a Wittgensteinian model, conceptual amelioration does not work by having philosophers dictate new meanings for our old words. Rather, the Wittgensteinian approach would enjoin to fight on the rough ground of 'serious politics', as Naomi Scheman (2011: 17–18) calls it, so that even if a person whose natal sex was male, they would count as a woman, once they have undergone the transition (or even when they simply self-identify as such). As remarked, this change in the relevant concepts would not consist in substituting new concepts for our old ones, but rather in extending the existing concepts to cover new, not previously envisaged cases, by expanding the criteria for inclusion within the relevant class. If we want our concepts to be more inclusive, we need to 'shift the ground', as Scheman puts it (2011: 35), from which they arise.

Of course, from a Wittgensteinian perspective (1953: 67–68) we may always redescribe the situation by saying that a nativist concept WOMAN has been replaced by a more inclusive one. Yet, this should not obscure the fact that these would be just temporal stages of a single, evolving concept, that we may want or need to latch onto for pragmatic purposes.

Still, the extension of the relevant concepts to new cases is made possible and brought about by certain changes in the social and political world, effected by serious political activism, where the agents are, typically, stakeholders and those of us who, while not being directly affected, share the hopes for a better future for marginalized members of our society.

Furthermore, this is not just how, typically, conceptual amelioration occurs – after all, characteristically even the law follows practice by updating according to relevant societal pressures. Rather, this is how amelioration *ought to occur*. For this mode of amelioration is of a piece with a democratic, non-authoritarian and non-paternalistic conception of how society works and improves itself.

5.2 'I Am a Woman'

There are two other important tools in a Wittgensteinian toolkit to be used in connection with issues about gender. First, the idea of an avowal, and the nature of the first-personal authority attached to it; second, the idea of a personal hinge. The former, as we saw in Section 1, consists in recognizing that it is by dint of the grammar of our language that we accord first-person authority to avowals of sensations and other mental states. Thus, we take subjects at their word when they avow pain or other mental states. Obviously, this does not mean that their avowals cannot ever be defeated, but only that, in the normal run of cases, when the subject is sincere and conceptually competent, we don't question their avowal of pain, or of a toothache, any more than we question a cry after an injury.[50]

Conversely, in the normal run of cases, third-personal doubts about avowals are legitimate only if there is reason to think that a subject is being insincere or lacks competence in using the relevant psychological vocabulary. Moreover, in the case of avowals of intentional mental states, such as beliefs and desires, self-deception may be another avenue for challenging first-personal authority.[51] Barring these cases, however, the onus is on the doubter to explain why their doubt is legitimate. In fact, it may easily turn out that it isn't. For instance, Borgoni (2019) discusses cases where a sexist co-worker challenges a woman's colleague's claim 'I *believe* that *A* is the best candidate for the job'. In such cases, the problem isn't that a woman's belief may be false because *A* may not be the best candidate for the job. Rather, it's to deny that she genuinely holds the belief she avows. However, given that, *ex hypothesi*, she is conceptually competent, sincere and not self-deceived, a grammatical account of first-personal authority can effectively explain why such challenges are not only morally problematic, as they are based on sexist prejudice, but also epistemically so, thus representing forms of testimonial injustice (Fricker 2007). For the speaker isn't accorded the credibility she deserves with respect to her own mind. Moreover, the hearer isn't acquiring knowledge (about their colleague's attitude regarding the candidate, and possibly her reasons for it) which would be at their disposal, if they weren't prejudiced. Finally, given that, *ex hypothesi*, there are no objective reasons for the hearer to doubt the speaker's sincerity, her linguistic competence, or lack of self-deception, their doubt is groundless and a manifestation of irrationality on their part.

Furthermore, in *On Certainty*, Wittgenstein allows for personal hinges, like 'My name is LW' (OC 328, 425, 470, 490–1, 567, 628, 656), or 'I am in England' (OC 420–423). That is, propositions which go without saying for each of us, and that share the characteristics of the more general hinges we discussed in Section 2, like the fact that 'I know' with respect to them plays a grammatical role and that doubt is excluded with respect to them. Clearly those statements aren't hinges for other people, who may be uncertain about our name, or our location.[52] Yet, the fact that they are hinges for us is reflected in the

[50] Nor does it mean that there cannot be what we may call 'third-personal' psychological *self*-ascriptions, arrived at by following third-personal epistemic methods, such as observation, inference to the best explanation, simulation, testimony, and so on. See Coliva (2016) for a discussion of third-personal self-knowledge.

[51] See Coliva (2016) for ample discussion of self-deception in the context of a Wittgenstein-inspired account of first-person authority over one's self-ascriptions of intentional mental states.

[52] Even though the relevant counterparts to those statements, regarding their own names and location, would be personal hinges for them.

fact that, in the normal run of cases, other people neither do, nor ought to challenge our pronouncements (assuming sincerity and conceptual mastery).

Now, psychological avowals and personal hinges aren't identical. For, at the very least, their subject-matter is different. Yet, they have certain features in common, for Wittgenstein, like the fact that 'I know' with respect to them plays a *grammatical* role (Section 1.2), and connectedly, that doubts about them would be excluded in the normal run of cases, albeit for only partially related reasons.[53]

Interestingly, among personal hinges Wittgenstein mentions 'I am a man/woman', OC 79–83:

> That I am a man and not a woman can be verified, but if I were to say I was a woman, and then tried to explain the error by saying I hadn't checked the statement, the explanation would not be accepted.
>
> The *truth* of my statements is the test of my *understanding* of these statements.
>
> That is to say: if I make certain false statements, it becomes uncertain whether I understand them.
>
> What counts as an adequate test of a statement belongs to logic. It belongs to the description of the language-game.
>
> The *truth* of certain empirical propositions belongs to our frame of reference.

Hence, 'I am a man', for Wittgenstein himself, is a hinge. That is, even if it has an *empirical* content, at least in context, it plays a *rule-like role* (OC 95), for him and his community. That is, *qua* hinge, a doubt about it would reveal a lack of understanding of the term 'man' and could not be supported by reasons.[54]

Still, it is part and parcel of Wittgenstein's views about hinges that they may be subject to change. This, arguably, is also the case with personal hinges related to one's gender. Thus, it may be that through a process of self-discovery, during which 'I am a man/woman' is very much like an ordinary empirical proposition for the subject, one ends up embracing a different hinge, in which one's avowed gender differs from one's natal sex. In other cases, in contrast, one's avowed gender may indeed be different from one's natal sex from very early on and this, in turn, may be a bedrock certainty for the subject (Moyal-Sharrock and Sandis 2024). The important point is that once 'I am a man/woman', based on self-identification, becomes a personal hinge, it is indubitable for the subject. That is also why, if spoken out loud by someone for whom it is a hinge, it would resemble an avowal, from a first-personal point of view.

[53] Sincerity and conceptual mastery are presupposed in both cases, while lack of self-deception would be presupposed only with respect to one's attitudinal avowals.

[54] Things would be otherwise if it didn't play a hinge-role and were considered merely an empirical proposition.

The next point to consider, however, is whether at the societal level 'I am a woman/man', based on self-identification, is treated as a hinge, such that subjects are accorded authority over their self-identifications, even when different from one's natal sex (granted sincerity, conceptual mastery, and lack of self-deception). Clearly, up until recently, and certainly at the time when Wittgenstein was writing, this wasn't the case.

Now, for Wittgenstein, 'what counts as an adequate test of a statement belongs to logic' (OC 82).[55] Thus, precluding one's own self-identification from being an adequate test of whether one is a man or a woman (or belongs to any other non-cis category), amounts to normatively excluding it from playing a role in the determination of a person's gender. It also precludes the self-identification from being taken at face value – just like a psychological avowal, in the normal run of cases – by other members of the community.

Armed with this idea we can now reframe current debates about the extension of WOMAN to trans women, and/or about non-binary identities as debates about renegotiating the hinges – that is, the rules of evidential significance – that will have to be operative when we are answering questions regarding a person's gender. On the one hand, there is a traditional hinge 'Gender is binary and coincident with one's natal sex', such that only the observation of genitalia at the time of birth counts in answering the question whether a person is a man or a woman. On the other hand, there is the more progressive hinge 'Gender isn't binary and isn't determined *solely* by one's natal sex', such that *also* non-cis self-identifications are allowed to play a role in answering that kind of question.

A hinge disagreement of this kind would involve which judgements would count as paradigmatically correct applications of that concept, and whether we take self-identifications to have the kind of authority we typically ascribe to psychological avowals and to socially recognized personal hinges. Furthermore, this will also impact various downstream judgments, such as deeming individuals who don't identify with their natal sex as having a psychiatric disorder; or else, accusing those who don't take self-identifications at face value, as a valid factor in determining gender, of being prejudiced against non-cis people, and thereby perpetrating a form of testimonial injustice by not taking these self-identifications at face value.

Importantly, it is noticeable that we are already operating differently from an epistemic point of view than in the past. At the time when Wittgenstein was writing, only the conservative hinge was operative, and there was no practice of

[55] 'Logic' is meant in the extended sense of grammatical norm.

asking people which pronoun others should use to refer to them. Nowadays, things have changed or are changing – surely not without opposition – especially in some Western societies. What used to be a societal hinge – the conservative one – is being demoted, and is highly contested, if not altogether replaced by the more progressive one.

5.3 Conclusions

As anticipated in Section 1.3, philosophers moved by the desire to ameliorate society, *qua* philosophers, are often bothered by Wittgenstein's alleged quietism – that is, the view that we can only describe our communal use of words. On this reading of Wittgenstein, it would not be appropriate for philosophers to engage in these battles, *qua* philosophers, and there wouldn't be anything specific that they could bring to the cause of ameliorating society.

It's doubtful that this is the correct description of what Wittgenstein was after. His quietism is much more apparent than real. In fact, if he was against theory, it was only in a specific sense of 'theory', mostly to be found in metaphysics and in foundationalist projects in epistemology. Roughly, Wittgenstein was against the kind of theory, *as applied to philosophy* – not to science – that vertically tries to ground more complex truths on a limited set of more fundamental ones, and that aims to unveil the hidden essence of phenomena (Coliva 2021b, 2024d). Moreover, his descriptivism, as we have been seeing, is only inimical to the idea that philosophy should (or could) revise or regiment linguistic uses.

However, Wittgenstein was not against a kind of theory, in philosophy (but also in anthropology or sociology) that tries to give us a perspicuous and synoptic presentation of the complex interrelations of our concepts and that brings to light differences which may go unnoticed under the superficial similarity of the words we use.

Furthermore, Wittgenstein coined or inspired several philosophical notions, such as 'family resemblance', 'language-game', 'form of life', 'hinge proposition', 'world-picture', and so on which, albeit not explicitly defined by him, do serve the theoretical purpose of understanding phenomena such as meaning, concepts, rules, justification, knowledge, and so on.

If the arguments in this section are roughly on the right track, notions like family resemblance, first-person avowal (with its inherent first-person authority), and of (personal) hinge proposition can serve as valuable theoretical tools for understanding conceptual change, particularly around the concept WOMAN. These conceptual tools can also shed light on debates about the role of self-identification in discussions of gender, while promoting epistemic justice – both hermeneutical and testimonial – by allowing individuals to use concepts (such as WOMAN) that better capture their lived experiences (when this is in fact the case), or to be taken at face value when they express their gender identity, irrespective of their natal sex. Clearly, a Wittgensteinian approach to these societal issues has much to recommend it.

References

Ashton, N. 2019 'The case for a feminist hinge epistemology', *Wittgenstein Studien* 10/1: 152–164.

Avnur, Y. and Scott-Kakures, D. 2015 'How irrelevant influences bias belief', *Philosophical Perspectives* 29/1: 7–39.

Baghramian, M. and Coliva, A. 2020 *Relativism*, New York, Routledge.

Baier, A. 1986 'Trust and antitrust', *Ethics* 96: 231–260.

Barnes, B. and Bloor, D. 1996 *Scientific Knowledge: A Sociological Analysis*, Chicago, University of Chicago Press.

Bettcher, T. 2012 'Trans women and the meaning of "woman"', in N. Power, R. Halwani, and A. Soble (eds.) *The Philosophy of Sex: Contemporary Readings*, New York, Rowman & Littlefield: 233–250.

Boncompagni, A. 2019 'Hinges, prejudices and radical doubters', *Wittgenstein Studien* 10/1: 165–182.

Boncompagni, A. 2024a 'Hermeneutical injustice and bisexuality: Toward new conceptual tools', *Hypatia* Published online 2024: 1–19. https://doi.org/10.1017/hyp.2024.28.

Boncompagni A. 2024b 'Prejudice in Testimonial Justification: A Hinge Account', *Episteme* 21/1:286–303

Borgoni, C. 2019 'Authority and attribution: The case of epistemic injustice in self-knowledge', *Philosophia* 47: 293–301.

Burge, T. 1993 'Content preservation', *Philosophical Review* 102: 457–488.

Butler, J. 1988 'Performative acts and gender constitution: An essay in phenomenology and feminist theory', *Theatre Journal* 40/4: 519–531.

Carnap, R. 1950 'Empiricism, semantics and ontology', *Revue Internationale de Philosophie* 4: 20–40.

Code, L. 1991 *What Can She Know? Feminist Theory and the Construction of Knowledge*, Ithaca, Cornell University Press.

Cohen, G. A. 2000 *If You're an Egalitarian, How Come You're So Rich*? Cambridge, MA, Harvard University Press.

Coliva, A. 2010 *Moore and Wittgenstein: Scepticism, Certainty and Common Sense*, London, Palgrave.

Coliva, A. 2013a 'Hinges and certainty: A Précis of *Moore and Wittgenstein: Scepticism, Certainty and Common Sense*', *Philosophia* 41: 1–12. https://doi.org/10.1007/s11406-012-9399-9.

Coliva, A. 2013b 'Replies', *Philosophia* 41: 81–96. https://doi.org/10.1007/s11406-012-9402-5.

Coliva, A. 2015 *Extended Rationality: A Hinge Epistemology*, London, Palgrave.

Coliva, A. 2016 *The Varieties of Self-Knowledge*, London, Palgrave.

Coliva, A. 2018 'What do philosophers do? Maddy, Moore (and Wittgenstein)', *International Journal for the Study of Skepticism* 8/3: 198–207.

Coliva, A. 2019 'Testimonial hinges', *Philosophical Issues* 29: 53–68.

Coliva, A. 2021a 'Stebbing, Moore (and Wittgenstein) on common sense and metaphysical analysis', *British Journal for the History of Philosophy* 29: 914–934.

Coliva, A. 2021b 'Doubts, philosophy, and therapy', *Midwest Studies in Philosophy* 45: 1–23.

Coliva, A. 2024a 'What do philosophers do? Maddy, Moore (and Wittgenstein) II', in S. Arbeiter and J. Kennedy (eds.) *The Philosophy of Penelope Maddy*, Dordrecht, Springer: 299–310.

Coliva, A. 2024b 'So one cannot say "There are objects" as one says "There are books": From *Tractatus* 4.1272 to Carnap, via *On Certainty* 35–37', in A. Pichler, E. Heinrich-Ramharter, and F. Stadler (eds.) *100 Years of Tractatus Logico-Philosophicus — 70 Years after Wittgenstein's Death: A Critical Assessment*, Berlin, De Gruyter: 303–318.

Coliva, A. 2024c 'Woman: Concept, prototype, and stereotype', *Social Epistemology*: 1–10. https://doi.org/10.1080/02691728.2024.2400551.

Coliva, A. 2024d 'Morphology and metaphilosophy: Goethe, Wittgenstein and Waismann', *Nordic Wittgenstein Review* 13: 1–23.

Coliva, A. 2025 *Social and Applied Hinge Epistemology*, New York, Oxfrod University Press.

Coliva, A. 2025a 'More and happier women: On the political significance of Wittgenstein and hinge epistemology', *Hypatia* 40: 426–442. https://doi.org/10.1017/hyp.2024.58.

Coliva, A. 2025b 'Hinge trust', *Philosophy and Phenomenological Research* 110/3:939–958. https://doi.org/10.1111/phpr.13142.

Coliva, A. 2025c 'Hysteria, hermeneutical injustice and conceptual engineering', *Social Epistemology* 39/2: 121–133. https://doi.org/10.1080/02691728.2024.2400089.

Coliva, A. 2025d 'Against quasi-fideism', Religions, 16, pp. 1–14. doi.org/10.3390/ rel16030365.

Coliva, A. and Palmira, M. 2020 'Hinge disagreement', in M. Kusch (ed.) *Social Epistemology and Epistemic Relativism*, New York, Routledge: 11–29.

Coliva, A. and Palmira, M. 2021 'Disagreement unhinged constitutivism-style', *Metaphilosophy* 52: 402–415.

Craig, E. 1991 *Knowledge and the State of Nature*, Oxford, Oxford University Press.

D'Cruz, J. 2020 'Trust and distrust', in J. Simon (ed.) *The Routledge Handbook of Trust and Philosophy*, New York, Routledge: xx–xxx.

Fogelin, R. 1985 'The logic of deep disagreements', *Informal Logic* 7: 1–8.

Fricker, E. 1994 'Against gullibility', in A. Chakrabarti and B. K. Matilal (eds.) *Knowing from Words*, Dordrecht, Kluwer: 125–161.

Fricker, M. 2007 *Epistemic Injustice: Power and Ethics of Knowing*, Oxford, Oxford University Press.

Fricker, M. 2008 'Scepticism and the genealogy of knowledge: Situating epistemology in time', *Philosophical Papers* 37/1: 27–50.

Goldberg, S. 2020 'Trust and reliance', in J. Simon (ed.) *The Routledge Handbook of Trust and Philosophy*, New York, Routledge: 97–108.

Greco, J. 2016 'Common knowledge', in A. Coliva and D. Moyal-Sharrock (eds.) *Hinge Epistemology*, Leiden, Brill: 237–278.

Greco, J. 2021 *The Transmission of Knowledge*, Cambridge, Cambridge University Press.

Hale, C. J. 1996 'Are lesbians women?', *Hypatia* 11/2: 94–121.

Hardin, R. 2002 *Trust and Trustworthiness*, New York, Russell Sage Foundation.

Haslanger, S. 2000 'What are we talking about? The semantics and politics of social kinds', *Hypatia* 20: 10–26.

Haslanger, S. 2012 *Resisting Reality*, Oxford, Oxford University Press.

Hawley, K. 2019 *Trust and Distrust*, Oxford, Oxford University Press.

Hay, C. 2020 *Think Like a Feminist: The Philosophy behind the Revolution*, New York, W. W. Norton.

Hertzberg, L. 1988 'On the attitude of trust', *Inquiry* 31/3: 307–322.

Hobbes, T. 1640 *The Elements of Law*, Oxford: Oxford University Press.

Holton, R. 1994 'Deciding to trust, coming to believe', *Australasian Journal of Philosophy* 72/1: 63–76.

Jones, K. 1996 'Trust as an affective attitude', *Ethics* 107/1: 4–25.

Kapusta, S. 2017 'Intersex diagnostics and prognostics: Imposing sex-predicate determinacy', *Topoi* 36: 539–548.

Lagerspetz, O. 1998 *Trust: The Tacit Demand*, Dordrecht, Kluwer.

Laugier, S., Provost, M., and Trächtler, J. 2022 (eds.) *Wittgenstein and Feminism*. Special Issue of the *Nordic Wittgenstein Review*. https://doi.org/10.15845/nwr.v0.

McFarlane, J. 2014 *Assessment Sensitivity: Relative Truth and Its Applications*, Oxford, Oxford University Press.

Mill, J. S. 1859 *On Liberty*, Oxford, Oxford University Press.

Mogensen, A. L. 2016 'Contingency anxiety and the epistemology of disagreement', *Pacific Philosophical Quarterly* 97/4: 590–611.

Moore, G. E. (ed.) 1925 'A defence of common sense', in *Philosophical Papers*, London, George Allen & Unwin: 32–45.

Moore, G. E. (ed.) 1939 'Proof of an external world', in *Philosophical Papers*, London, George Allen & Unwin: 127–150.

Moyal-Sharrock, D. 2004 *Understanding Wittgenstein's* On Certainty, London, Palgrave.

Moyal-Sharrock, D. and Sandis, C. 2024 *Real Gender: A Cis Defence of Trans Realities*, London, Polity.

Newman, J. H. 1870 *An Essay in Aid of the Grammar of Assent*, Cambridge, Cambridge University Press.

Nguyen, C. T. 2022 'Trust as an unquestioning attitude', *Oxford Studies in Epistemology*, Oxford, Oxford University Press: 214–244.

O'Connor, P. 2008 *Morality and Our Complicated Form of Life: Feminist Wittgensteinian Metaethics*, University Park, Penn State University Press.

Obertello, L. 2000 *La grammatica dell'assenso di John Henry Newman*, Milano, Jaca Books.

Oswald, J. 1766–1772 *An Appeal to Common Sense in Behalf of Religion*, in J. Fieser and J. Oswald (eds.) *Scottish Common Sense Philosophy: Sources and Origins*, Sterling, Thoemmes Press.

Pascal, B. 1958 *Pensées*, New York, Dutton.

Pederneschi, A. 2024 'An analysis of bias and distrust in social hinge epistemology', *Philosophical Psychology* 37/1: 258–277.

Pritchard, D. 2015 *Epistemic Angst: Radical Skepticism and the Groundlessness of Our Believing*, Princeton, Princeton University Press.

Pritchard, D. 2023 'Hinge commitments and trust', *Synthese* 202/5: 1–20.

Quine, W. V. O. 1951 'Two dogmas of empiricism', *The Philosophical Review* 60/1: 20–43.

Reid, T. 1764 *An Inquiry into the Human Mind on the Principles of Common Sense*, Cambridge, Cambridge University Press, 1997.

Rosch, E. and Mervis, C. B. 1975 'Family resemblances: Studies in the internal structure of categories', *Cognitive Psychology* 7: 573–605.

Scheman, N. 2011 *Shifting Ground: Knowledge and Reality, Transgression and Trustworthiness*, Oxford, Oxford University Press.

Scheman, N. and O'Connor, P. 2002 (eds.) *Feminist Interpretations of Ludwig Wittgenstein*, University Park, Penn State University Press.

Schönbaumsfeld, G. 2023 *Wittgenstein and Religious Belief*, Cambridge, Cambridge University Press.

Simpson, T. 2012 'What is trust?', *Pacific Philosophical Quarterly* 93: 550–569.

Stebbing, S. 1932 'The method of analysis in metaphysics', *Proceedings of the Aristotelian Society* 33: 65–94.

Stebbing, S. 1937 *Philosophy and the Physicists*, London, Methuen.

Stern, R. 2017 '"Trust is basic": Løgstrup on the priority of trust', in P. Faulkner and T. Simpson (eds.) *The Philosophy of Trust*, Oxford, Oxford University Press: 272–293.

Stoljar, N. 1995 'Essence, identity and the concept of woman', *Philosophical Topics* 23/2: 261–293.

Stoljar, N. 2011 'Different women: Gender and the realism-nominalism debate', in C. Witt (ed.) *Feminist Metaphysics*, Dordrecht, Springer: 27–46.

Tanesini, A. 2004 *Wittgenstein: A Feminist Interpretation*, Cambridge, Polity.

Waismann, F. 1965 *The Principles of Linguistic Philosophy*, New York, St. Martin's Press.

White, R. 2010 'You just believe that because . . . ', *Philosophical Perspectives* 24/1: 573–615.

Williams, B. 2002 *Truth and Truthfulness: An Essay in Genealogy*, Princeton, Princeton University Press.

Williams, M. 2004 'Wittgenstein, truth and certainty', in M. Kölbel and B. Weiss (eds.) *Wittgenstein's Lasting Significance*, London, Routledge: 249–284.

Winch, P. 1958 *The Idea of a Social Science and Its Relation to Philosophy*, London, Routledge.

Wittgenstein, L. 1921 *Tractatus Logico-Philosophicus*, Oxford, Blackwell.

Wittgenstein, L. 1953 *Philosophical Investigations*, Oxford, Blackwell.

Wittgenstein, L. 1956 *Remarks on the Foundations of Mathematics*, Oxford, Blackwell.

Wittgenstein, L. 1966 *Lectures and Conversations on Aesthetics, Psychology and Religious Belief*, Oxford, Blackwell.

Wittgenstein, L. 1969 *On Certainty*, Oxford, Blackwell.

Wittgenstein, L. 1980 *Culture and Value*, Oxford, Blackwell.

Wittgenstein, L. 1993 *Remarks on Frazer's* The Golden Bough, in *Philosophical Occasions*, Indianapolis, Hackett: 119–155.

Wright, C. 1985 Facts and Certainty. *Proceedings of the British Academy* 71: 429–472.

Wright, C. 1992 *Truth and Objectivity*, Boston, Harvard University Press.

Wright, C. 2004 'Warrant for nothing (and foundations for free)?', *The Supplementary Volume of the Aristotelian Society* 78: 167–212.

Acknowledgements

Special thanks to David G. Stern for supporting this project throughout its various stages and for many valuable comments on the first draft of this Element. I am also particularly grateful to Edward (Ted) Mark for his editorial work on the penultimate draft of the manuscript. Many thanks are due also to two anonymous reviewers for their many insightful comments that helped me improve the manuscript. I would like to thank all colleagues and students who have given me feedback on earlier versions of this Element, or on one or more of its parts: Robert Audi, Yuval Avnur, Maria Baghramian, Anna Boncompagni, Felice Cimatti, Jason D'Cruz, Nevia Dolcini, Louis Doulas, Elizabeth Fricker, John Greco, Pamela Hieronymi, Vito Alberto Lippolis, Danièle Moyal-Sharrock, Michele Palmira, Anna Pederneschi, Duncan Pritchard, Constantine Sandis, Genia Schönbaumsfeld, Ernest Sosa, Giorgio Volpe, Michael Williams, and Luca Zanetti. Thanks are also due to all students in attendance at my graduate seminar on Wittgenstein and social epistemology, in Fall 2024, at the University of California, Irvine.

Cambridge Elements

The Philosophy of Ludwig Wittgenstein

David G. Stern

University of Iowa

David G. Stern is a Professor of Philosophy and a Collegiate Fellow in the College of Liberal Arts and Sciences at the University of Iowa. His research interests include history of analytic philosophy, philosophy of language, philosophy of mind, and philosophy of science. He is the author of *Wittgenstein's Philosophical Investigations: An Introduction* (Cambridge University Press, 2004) and *Wittgenstein on Mind and Language* (Oxford University Press, 1995), as well as more than 50 journal articles and book chapters. He is the editor of *Wittgenstein in the 1930s: Between the 'Tractatus' and the 'Investigations'* (Cambridge University Press, 2018) and is also a co-editor of the *Cambridge Companion to Wittgenstein* (Cambridge University Press, 2nd edition, 2018), *Wittgenstein: Lectures, Cambridge 1930–1933, from the Notes of G. E. Moore* (Cambridge University Press, 2016) and *Wittgenstein Reads Weininger* (Cambridge University Press, 2004).

About the Series

This series provides concise and structured introductions to all the central topics in the philosophy of Ludwig Wittgenstein. The Elements are written by distinguished senior scholars and bright junior scholars with relevant expertise, producing balanced and comprehensive coverage of the full range of Wittgenstein's thought.

Cambridge Elements

The Philosophy of Ludwig Wittgenstein

Elements in the Series

Wittgenstein on Forms of Life
Anna Boncompagni

Wittgenstein on Criteria and Practices
Lars Hertzberg

Wittgenstein on Religious Belief
Genia Schönbaumsfeld

Wittgenstein and Aesthetics
Hanne Appelqvist

Style, Method and Philosophy in Wittgenstein
Alois Pichler

Wittgenstein on Realism and Idealism
David R. Cerbone

Wittgenstein and Ethics
Anne-Marie Søndergaard Christensen

Wittgenstein and Russell
Sanford Shieh

Wittgenstein on Music
Eran Guter

Wittgenstein on Knowledge and Certainty
Danièle Moyal-Sharrock and Duncan Pritchard

Wittgenstein on Colour, 1916–1950
Andrew Lugg

Wittgenstein and Social Epistemology
Annalisa Coliva

A full series listing is available at: www.cambridge.org/EPLW

For EU product safety concerns, contact us at Calle de José Abascal, 56–1°,
28003 Madrid, Spain or eugpsr@cambridge.org.

www.ingramcontent.com/pod-product-compliance
Ingram Content Group UK Ltd.
Pitfield, Milton Keynes, MK11 3LW, UK
UKHW022143080726
473066UK00010B/735

* 9 7 8 1 0 0 9 5 5 1 3 4 2 *